# *THE BOOK OF JOB AND BIBLICAL CHRONOLOGY*

## A CRITICAL LOOK AT THE AGE OF THE EARTH

**A Petroleum Geologist declares:**
**"The earth is not millions or billions – but thousands of years old!"**

**FRANK CRAWFORD**

Copyright © 2021 by Frank Crawford
June, 2021
All Rights Reserved
Printed in the United States of America

## Disclaimer

The author of this work has quoted the writers of many articles and books. This does not mean that the author endorses or recommends the works of others, though he may speak highly of their research and contributions to the subject at hand. If the author quotes someone, it does not mean that he agrees with all of the author's tenets, statements, or words, whether in the work quoted or any other work of the author. There has been no attempt to alter the meaning of the quotes.

Earth Sciences & Religion with Interpretation

**ISBN: 978-1-7371005-2-2**

All Scripture quotations are from the King James 1611 Bible.

No part of this book may be reproduced without the expressed consent of the publisher, except for brief quotes, whether by electronic, photocopying, recording, or information storage and retrieval systems.

Address All Inquiries To:
THE OLD PATHS PUBLICATIONS, Inc.
142 Gold Flume Way
Cleveland, Georgia, U.S.A.

Web: www.theoldpathspublications.com
E-mail: TOP@theoldpathspublications.com

**COVER PICTURE**: A View to the north along the thrust-faulted Kananaskis Range toward Three Sisters Mt. (2936 m) from the top of Mt. Sparrowhawk (3121 m), Canadian Rockies taken by Frank Crawford.

# DEDICATION

To the Memory of my Mother, Elizabeth Crawford.

## Acknowledgments

The author would like to thank Dr. and Mrs. H. D. Williams for reviewing the manuscript and making it fit for publication. A great debt of gratitude is due the instructors and students in the Graphic Arts Department of the Southern Alberta Institute of Technology for drafting the figures on Adobe Illustrator as part of their volunteer student project work. Mr. Ferdinand Gojo transferred the figures from the 2005 SAIT digital files to a format compatible for copying into the text of the book. Cora Gojo kindly helped with editing on Adobe illustrator. The late Dr. Herb Teitz, my friend and mentor, encouraged me to observe, to remember, to compare; and gave me an opportunity to work on a project that greatly helped develop my career as a petroleum exploration geologist. Mr. Ray Strom, owner of Calgary Rock and Materials Services, Inc. has kindly provided material and advice on dinosaur fossils and young earth creation studies. Bruce Bartlett generously lent me creation science references useful in my research. Harry Nibourg of the Big Valley Creation Science Museum in Big Valley, Alberta, supplied useful advice and audio-visual materials on creation. I have a debt of gratitude to Brother Larry Jones whose words of encouragement concerning the original manuscript of this book helped motivate me to eventually consider publishing it. Genevieve Occena provided computer assistance. Special thanks to my grandniece Julia Occena for her help on the computer and questions as I worked on this book.

# FORWARD

In 1972, I graduated as a geologist from a Canadian University. In my nearly six years of study there was no mention of God or the Bible in any of my courses. Below is a sample of the kind of teaching that is crippling the minds of modern day students in our nation's schools and universities. It came from a college text book that was recommended to my class as a mathematical explanation of geological processes.

> "Hutton is acknowledged as the father of modern geology not for the uniformitarian doctrine alone. He also freed geological thinking once and for all from the cramping influence of clerical teaching---hitherto unchallenged for over a thousand years---to the effect that time, inaugurated at the Creation, occupied the excessively narrow span of some 6000 years. Geology owes its peculiar and singular flavor to the pervasive role of time, whose total span, compared with that of written history, is vast." (Turner, F., and Verhoogen, J., 1970, The Earth: An Introduction to Physical Geology, p.13)

The subjects I studied were many and varied in the Geology Department, later to become the Department of Earth Sciences. I finished my second degree specializing in subsurface stratigraphy and carbonate/evaporite sedimentation. Never once did I question or give serious thought to the age dates given by my professors to explain the geological features observed in the nearby Rocky Mountains and around the world. Throughout my petroleum geology career I would have an opportunity to work in many of these areas and become familiar with their sedimentary basins. Yet, never once in a span of over 40 years did anyone I worked with question the Darwinian evolutionary philosophy implanted by their secular education concerning the age of the earth being billions of years and the geological processes and their rock record millions and hundreds of millions of years old. Everyone accepted the uniformitarian concept that states, "the present is the key to the past," and went on with their geological work in that context.

While in Grad School in 1970-71 I took a course in Precambrian Geology. In it the professor described radiometric dating in relation to the age of the earth. At the time I wondered about the many assumptions made for the various math formulae used in the time "clocks" for computing the millions and billions of years of time invoked to explain geological processes and the earth's age. Not until many years later did I realize the evolutionary bias and philosophy that had been imposed upon science regarding the age and origin of things. We students were being indoctrinated in a mixture of assumptions, guesses, and narratives or paradigms imposed by professors who had been educated in the same way.

I remember working as a field geologist observing outcrops during the late 1960s, and as a subsurface carbonate specialist, studying cores and chip samples in detail from the Western Canadian Sedimentary Basin. Never once did I observe any aberrant forms in the fossil record. Everything was orderly and arranged according to the species or kinds, that is, corals were corals, brachiopods varied but were always brachiopods, blue green algae were always blue green algae. Changes in form of certain fossils reflected variation in the depositional environment but they were still within their kinds or well defined groups. Even microflora and microfauna were ordered in a way that they could be categorized and studied in an orderly way. We contracted such studies many times in our exploration projects. Though I did not think of it then these fossilized physical organisms, though varying within their kinds (genera) did not change from one "kind" to another kind. What I was witnessing, although ignorant of its import, was the Biblical creation mentioned in Genesis Chapter 1.

> *"And God said, Let the earth bring forth grass, the herb yielding seed, and the fruit tree yielding fruit after his kind, whose seed is in itself, upon the earth: and it was so. And the earth brought forth grass, and herb yielding seed after his kind, and the tree yielding fruit, whose seed was in itself, after his kind: and God saw that it was good."* (Genesis 1:11-12)

> *"And God created great whales, and every living creature that moveth, which the waters brought forth abundantly, after their kind, and every winged fowl after his kind: and God saw that it was good."* (Genesis 1:21)

Only after becoming a Christian in 1981 did I personally begin to read the Bible and understand it as a supernatural Book written by a supernatural God. Little by little I saw the enormous gap between what I had been taught at university and what God's Word said happened. I also began to see places in the Bible where a number of geological processes and subjects were described accurately in only a few sentences or a short passage of scripture - and all within the context of thousands of years of existing human civilization and not geological ages. This correlation prompted me to take note of these things and make the connection from existing scientific publications and literature. Slowly I began to develop an earth history view very different from my university education and consistent with the Biblical chronology in thousands and not millions of years. The Old Testament Book of Job was the most informative in this regard. It became the basis for much of the material found in the following chapters. Other books of the Bible were used where applicable. Most people dismiss outright these time frame assertions and say they are impossible. But the Word of God reminds man in Luke 1:37 and elsewhere that, ***"For with God nothing shall be impossible."*** I now conclude that if God says it, I believe it, and that settles it! I do not claim to have figured out all of what God has done. I have applied my secular experience with my Bible study to try and show that the Bible is true and has the answer to the earth's origin and physical processes. I have not provided the total picture of what God has done. No man can; and no man ever will. God has said so in Ecclesiastes 8:17. But God has provided enough information in His Word to refute the false theory of evolution and the equally false teaching that this earth has undergone millions of years of evolution (Darwinian or otherwise) and is billions of years old. Please follow with me through the Biblical interpretation of an earth history and geological chronology far different from what is being currently taught at secular academic institutions around the world, nearly every one of which has rejected the Word of God as truth. Many other scientists have written on this subject of Biblical creation and their works may be easily sought out and read.

I am now an aged man and retired from my profession. I wrote the original manuscript in the early 2000s but publication seemed very remote. Also, there was little support or encouragement to carry the work further. With SAIT's help I was able to get the figures professionally drafted in 2005. More recently I have had the time – thanks to COVID-19 – to revive the effort into bringing this material into print. With the kind help of Dr. Williams at Old Paths Publications I have been able to do so. I am grateful to God for bringing me back to this project and raising up helpful souls to advance the original manuscript into a published book.

The two Appendices at the end of the book contain the salvation message from the Bible. I believe it is indispensable to any work of a Biblical nature including the subject of creation science. The gospel message is probably the most important part of this work. The patriarch Job is mentioned worldwide as a man who had patience in the face of extreme trials and suffering. Underlying this man's character was an immovable faith in God. It sustained him when all other sources of support vanished. He speaks of a Savior – his personal redeemer – prefiguring the Lord Jesus Christ who came and shed His blood on the cross as an atonement for a lost and dying world nearly two millennia after Job's time.

Today we see a secular materialist world that has shut out God, and crucified its Creator and Savior, the Son of God. Jesus Christ is the Creator who you will read about in the following chapters. He went to the cross to die for our sins. Yet, the Bible and its divine Author are denigrated and ignored as if He did not exist. In 2021, this rebellion is reaching epic proportions, and it is only a matter of time before God brings judgment on a Christ-denying world. Dear Reader, I ask you to examine closely Job's Savior and Redeemer and consider your own never-dying soul in the light of eternity. For the God that cannot lie promised that He would save the repentant sinner who puts his faith and trust in His only begotten Son, the Lord Jesus Christ! The only other alternative is spending eternity in Hell which Job and his generation believed in so long ago, and which Jesus preached about more than heaven.

# TABLE OF CONTENTS

# INTRODUCTION

Modern science has made a grave mistake in saying that the processes operating on the earth today took place at the same rate as in the past, through which the belief in long time periods of millions and billions of years became established. Darwin's theory of evolution sprung out of this concept of vast ages of time and accounts for widespread acceptance of the Humanist religion in the 20th and 21st centuries. This entire problem began first with the deliberate rejection of Biblical chronology by a select group of atheists during the latter part of the 18th Century and onward into the 19th Century. Their teachings caught on slowly at first but exploded after the 1850's following the publishing of Darwin's *"On the Origin of Species"* in 1859. Pretty soon even many Christians were being misled into doubting the Genesis account of Creation by the so-called great advances in science. Theistic evolution and the Gap theory caught on which said God started it all but evolution took over using long periods of time different from the Bible's teaching. With the discovery of radioactivity at the end of the 19th Century and the application of radiometric 'dating' (called geochronology), geologists finally thought they had found the tool to measure the absolute age of the earth in millions and billions of years, confirming their earlier assumption of vast periods of time to account for the worldwide geological rock record comprising the so-called Geologic Column. With each successive 'scientific breakthrough' man was being led further away from God and belief in His Word. It seems that God has allowed man to become snared by his own intellect, by believing a series of lies which he has himself invented. All of these scientific 'advances' are based upon assumptions which are biased already toward a worldview or narrative that people want to believe; that is, there is no God, man is only an animal on the evolutionary ladder and everything we see today has developed by chance over long periods of geologic time. According to this teaching nothing very extraordinary has ever happened during the history of the earth; certainly nothing like the Flood mentioned in the Bible. Everything has just continued along slowly like today for millions and millions of years. It is purposeless and subject wholly to chance and natural (material) influences. Scripture accurately depicts the philosophy which prevails in our society today in 2 Peter 3: 3-6.

> *"Knowing this first, that there shall come in the last days scoffers, walking after their own lusts, And saying, Where is the promise of his coming? for since the fathers fell asleep, all things continue as they were from the beginning of the creation. For this they are willingly are ignorant of, that by the word of God the heavens were of old, and the earth standing out of the water and in the water: Whereby the world that then was, being overflowed with water, perished:"*

The AV 1611 Bible provides the answer to today's misconceptions in the earth sciences. It shines the light needed for our understanding of the age of the earth and the geological processes that shaped what we see today concerning continental drift, seafloor spreading, mountain belts, the fossil record, sedimentary deposits, glaciation, seafloor and the origin of man. It is authoritative in matters of science.

> "The Bible is scientifically true, although it is not a book of science." (Rockwood, Pastor P., F., The People's Gospel Hour broadcast, Halifax, Nova Scotia)

> "It is wisdom to recognize the Creator. It is wisdom to recognize His founding of the earth and His establishing of the heavens (Proverbs 3:19-20). All the different theories man holds do not matter; the simple facts in these two verses are the ones important to wisdom. That does not mean that we shouldn't study all the factors involved or the scientific research being done to prove the biblical statements in Genesis one. But neither does it mean that we need to go beyond these two verses. **Simple is good!** (Snyder, D., 2013, The Seven Pillars of Wisdom: Proverbs 1-9)

**Figures 1 and 16** should be examined together in understanding why earth history has followed the pattern of Biblical chronology. Man, God's highest created being, lived in a perfect world without sin or decay. Man's fall in the Garden of Eden, ushered in sin and death, and the whole of creation suffered as a result. Decay set in fulfilling the Second Law of Thermodynamics. This fall affected both mankind and the natural laws governing the universe, including the geological processes shaping the earth. Sin came to a climax in the first civilization; and God brought Noah's Flood to cleanse the earth and start afresh. The Flood judgment was an act of mercy to preserve mankind. Following the Flood and immediate Post-Flood period, God divided the earth, and in doing so separated man on different continents, again slowing down the spiritual entropy or decline that would eventually plunge the human race under divine judgment. We are nearing that judgment today. But God's mercy and grace are still giving individual people the opportunity to repent of their sin and be saved. The connection between the spiritual and natural dimensions are very real and God is in complete control. But He has left man with a free will to choose who to believe and who to serve. It is the writer's hope that this work might persuade some to serve Jesus Christ in whom is life everlasting. Please read on.

**Figure 1** presents a summary overview of earth history based upon secular geology and the Biblical chronology. It provides a synthesis of geological evidence from all available earth science studies, subsurface drilling and seismic correlations to create a chart of worldwide relative sea level from the Precambrian to the present day. The main phases of relative sea level correlate easily to the Biblical chronology. They comprise three megacycles: namely, Megacycle 1; The Creation continental crust – Early Precambrian era, and Megacycle 2; Noah's Flood sequence – Late Precambrian and Paleozoic eras, and Megacycle 3; Peleg's days – the "earth divided" – comprising the Mesozoic and Cenozoic eras, up to the end of the Pliocene epoch, after which the Pleistocene epoch with its glaciation led up to modern times. The Early Precambrian continental crust was formed at Creation approximately 4004 B.C. It was the living surface of the world civilization for the first 1658 years of human history until the time of Noah's Flood when the fountains of the great deep were broken up and the world was inundated with subterranean and rain waters to above the tops of the mountains. Noah's Flood occurred on 2348 B.C. (1658 A.C.) and lasted one year. Mankind and all living, breathing creatures were utterly and absolutely destroyed during the Flood; only marine life and the land plants' seeds survived outside the ark. All other living, breathing creatures and insects were preserved alive on the ark to re-populate the world after the waters subsided. Nothing at all remained of the Pre-Flood world with its millions of people and flourishing fowl and land creatures. The earth was cleansed and reshaped completely by the Flood. Noah, his wife, his three sons and their three wives survived to repopulate the 'New World.' The Flood and immediate Post-Flood world occupies the Late Precambrian and Paleozoic eras of the geologic record, a period of about one hundred years (2348 to 2247 B.C.). Noah left the ark sometime during the middle Paleozoic period when the earth had dried. By "dried," means that sufficient land area had been exposed and made accessible and livable to creatures leaving the ark at God's command (Genesis 8:15-19). Paleozoic seas continued in basins on the world's landmasses that coalesced to form the supercontinent Pangaea that was still intact at the end of the Permian period, 225 million years ago according to secular geology. Animals moved out rapidly from the ark to repopulate the cleansed earth to the four corners of the Post-Flood world later in the Paleozoic period. Mankind followed a short time later after being dispersed by God's judgment from Babel near the onset of the third megacycle, Peleg's days.

This paper does not deal specifically with the Late Precambrian and Paleozoic except to say that it records Noah's Flood and the Post-Flood period up to the "days of Peleg" when the earth was divided. The Late Precambrian notably lacks apparent sea level cyclicity internally and has a near uniform profile somewhat like an estuarine fill the writer has observed in younger sedimentary sequences. The Paleozoic is highly cyclical reaching a maximum level of the seas in the Devonian Period with waters gradually dropping to their lowest level in the late Permian before Pangaea began to break apart. Discrete ecosystems varying from exposed land areas to supratidal and intertidal conditions grading into shallow marine shelf and reef environments bordering a deep-water basin were identified by the writer in the Middle Devonian of Northern Alberta, Canada. Local sub-aqueous shelf 'meadows' of finger-like *Amphipora*, with stunted and robust growth forms, indicated restricted and normal marine salinities (Crawford, F., MSc. Thesis, U. of Calgary, 1972). These kinds of cyclical deposits in the Paleozoic indicate that discrete sedimentary basins remained after the Flood with accelerated rates of clastic (sand/silt/shale) and carbonate (limestone/shale) deposition far beyond what we see in today's world. The same type of sedimentation continued through the Mesozoic era and Tertiary Period, up to and including the Quaternary Pleistocene glaciation. They occurred in both clastic (sandstone/shale, etc.) and carbonate (limestone, etc.) depositional environments.

The Permian "great extinction" represents the end of Megacycle 2 at about 2247 B.C., about 100 years after the Flood. The Permian period records the lowest sea level following the Flood, and a time of extreme stress on all living creatures. According to secular scientists about 99% of all living species became extinct during the Permian. A remarkable paleontological find in Lower Permian rocks in New

Mexico shows that land animals had already reached the western part of Pangaea by this time. They are found during a period of worldwide dropping sea level and are, therefore, interpreted to be Post-Flood, not part of the peak flooding of the earth that occurred earlier in the Paleozoic. Some of these fossilized footprints are fowl and mammalian calling completely into question Darwinian evolutionary theory.

> "New Mexico paleontologist Jerry MacDonald (has identified) fossilized footprints and trackways of animals of all kinds, sizes and dispositions – walking, darting, swerving, pouncing – on an ancient muddy shoreline with raindrop prints. They include amphibians, centipedes, reptiles and creatures paleontologists call "problematica;" namely, a 3-toed creature that took a few steps, then disappeared, as though it took off and flew, and unusually large, deep and scary-looking footprints, each with five arched toe marks, like nails – that look just like bear tracks. Mammals or birds should have "evolved" after the Permian period. MacDonald suspects conventional theories about Permian times will end up being revised, perhaps extensively, by his finds." (Stewart, D., July, 1992, Petrified footprints: a puzzling parade of Lower Permian beasts, Smithsonian)

FIGURE ONE, NEXT PAGE

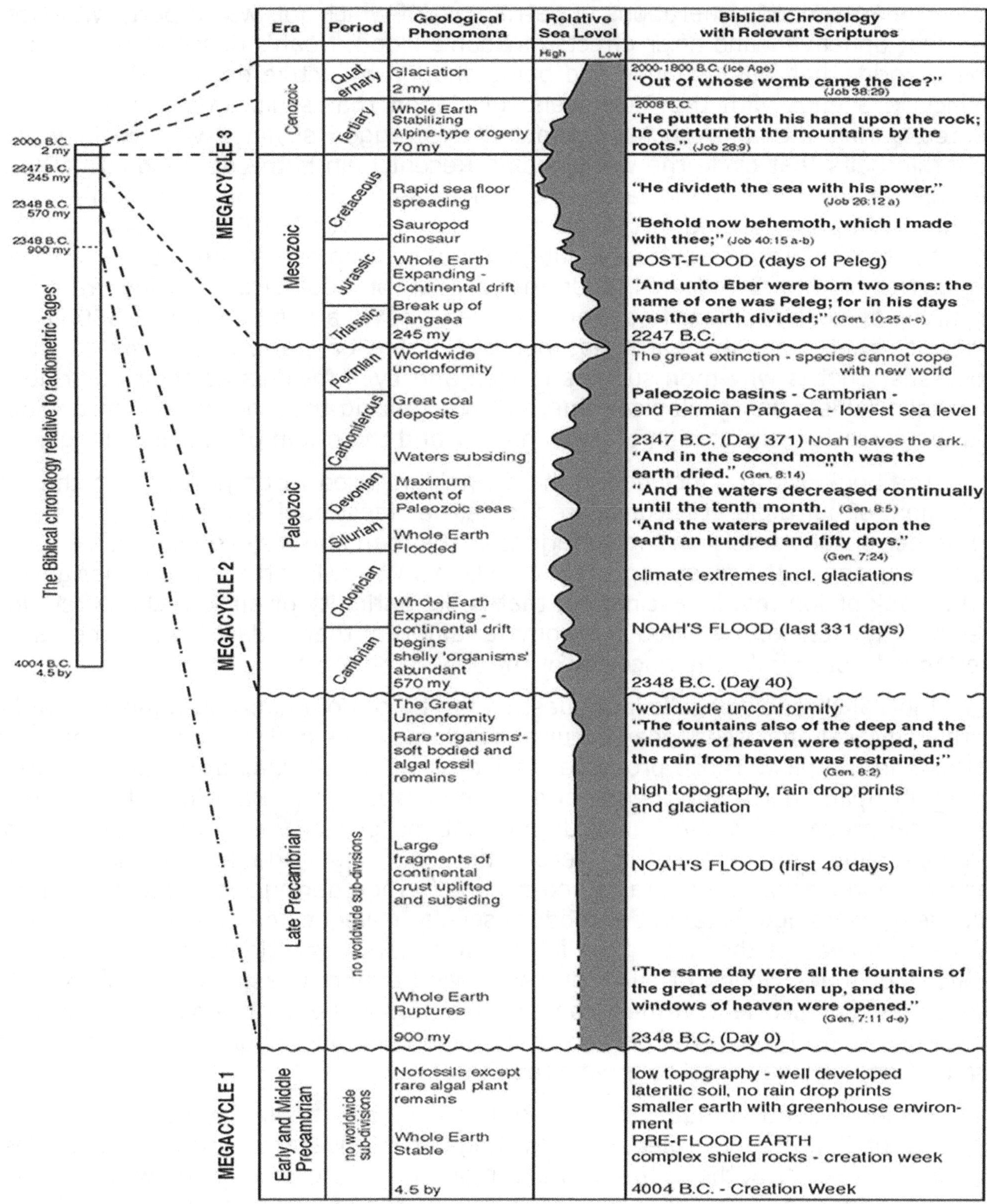


**Figure 1:**

The composite picture of earth history based upon the Biblical chronology relative seal level curve from Shell Oil, 1990 (see **Figure 16**)

The Post-Flood generations of patriarchs, of which Job was a part, witnessed the great upheavals and after-effects of Noah's Flood. Noah's descendants entered a new world, that was dynamic and being shaped by active geological processes. Megacycle 3 ends with the Pleistocene glaciation that sculptured the mountains created during the time of Peleg and left the ragged skylines we see in young mountain belts that circle the world today. Recent man is the descendant of Noah and his family who repopulated the earth after the Flood. Mankind's rapid technological progress and increased population, to over 7 billion persons in 2021, indicates that another catastrophic judgment is nearing as prophesied in the Bible. Megacycles 2 and 3 followed a dramatic path of geological entropy from the beginning of the Flood Year to the end of Peleg's days, a period of about 350 years; and since that time, the earth has become stable or static in regards to these processes. That is why men such as Hutton and Lyell formulated their doctrine of uniformitarianism and geological time, not recognizing that the Biblical chronology was the correct interpretation of earth history and the origin of all living things.

The Book of Job is included in the divinely inspired writings that form the Old Testament of our Bible. It is considered to be the oldest book in the Bible. Normally, the reader of Job centers on the sufferings of the man and his eventual deliverance. His story is one of the most encouraging in God's Word. But there is another aspect of the Book of Job that is fascinating, that is, its antiquity or ancient character. Job lived shortly after Noah's Flood in a world far different than today. His lifetime partly overlapped Abraham's, the ancestor of the Jewish nation.

Biblical chronology calls into question the theory of uniformitarianism, that is, earth's physical processes today occur at the same rates and in the same measures as those in the past. Those processes include seafloor spreading, continental drift, mountain uplift, earth subsidence and sedimentation. The Book of Job describes geological processes within hundreds and not millions of years. Rates of seafloor spreading and continental drift were orders of magnitude higher than today. Cenozoic and Mesozoic mountains and oceans formed during Job's lifetime and not millions of years ago as taught in modern secular colleges and universities **(Figure 1)**. He also lived at the same time as the dinosaurs, and witnessed them in their habitat. Job's description of earth processes and extinct beasts is far too accurate to have been an accident. It must come from a personal eyewitness account and his knowledge shared with other patriarchs that had been born shortly after the time of Noah's Flood and had lived to great ages thereafter.

Modern scientists must carefully study relevant portions of the Bible, including the Book of Job, and not reject these writings as exaggerated and fanciful stories. We need to take back the faith that Darwin and his successors stole away from us. Profound scientific truths are revealed in few words in Scripture because it is the authoritative Word of God. Today we will look at some of these passages in a book entitled, ***"The Book of Job and Biblical Chronology: A Critical Look at the Age of the Earth."***

There are several Scriptural scientific evidences for the ancient character of this book. They are interrelated and occur in perfect harmony with one another. Each example is described first with respect to the Bible and then compared to modern secular writings. Together they concur and provide compelling evidence that Scripture and the earth sciences are in perfect agreement. Before we look at the Book of Job and other Bible evidence for a young earth I would like to make a few qualifying statements concerning science and the Bible, and underline them with some verses of Scripture. Firstly, man can never find out the workings of God to perfection, even using the Bible and secular science. Secondly, man may search the Scriptures and find in them profound scientific truths, but only as far as God will allow him. Thirdly, there is no limit to God's power and workings.

> *"Then I beheld all the work of God, that a man cannot find out the work that is done under the sun: but though a man labour to seek it out, yet he shall not find it; yea further; though a wise man think to know it, yet shall he not be able to find it."* (Ecclesiastes 8:17)
>
> *"The secret things belong unto the LORD our God: but those things which are revealed belong unto us and to our children for ever, that we may do all the words of this law."* (Deuteronomy 29:29)
>
> *"For with God nothing shall be impossible."* (Luke 1:37)

Martin Luther said, "When the Scriptures speak, God speaks." Rejecting this wisdom is the norm today; and it is fatal spiritually and scientifically. Although the Bible is not a science textbook *per se*; when it speaks, true science will conform to its teachings and precepts. We must find how science fits the Bible and not the other way around. Man is finite and fallible; God's Word is infinite and true.

# CHAPTER 1

## THE BOOK OF JOB: ITS CENTRAL CHARACTER AND SETTING

The life span of man was much longer in the Pre-Flood world. Ages of eight to nine hundred years were common before God destroyed the world in Noah's day. Methuselah, the oldest man, lived to be nine hundred and sixty-nine years of age. Longevity began to decrease markedly following the deluge since the protective shield of atmospheric water vapor had condensed and fallen as rain during the first forty days. Men born into the New World lived much shortened lives. Arphaxad was born two years after the Flood and was four hundred and thirty-eight years old at his death. A major drop in life expectancy took place in the generation of Peleg, who died at an age of only two hundred and thirty-nine years. Later patriarchs lived progressively younger lives with few exceptions. By the time of Moses man's days were three score and ten years, and four score or a little more if given strength. It has remained so until today.

The Book of Job is set in an area known for the earliest of human history. Noah, Shem, Ham and Japheth and their wives left the ark in the mountains of Ararat near the border of Armenia and modern-day northeastern Turkey. The land of Uz lay to the south of Ararat in modern-day Iraq, Jordan and Saudi Arabia.

*"There was a man in the land of Uz, whose name was Job;"* (Job 1:1)

The Old Scofield Bible notes describe *"the land of Uz"* as follows:

"A region at the south of Edom, and west of the Arabian desert, extending to Chaldea."

Job lived in the Aramean part of the Chaldean Empire because he is described as one of *"the men of the east." (Job 1:3f pt.)* That would be in Mesopotamia, the area of the Tigris and Euphrates rivers. Job was also familiar with other parts of the Middle East. Chapter 40 indicates he had seen the ancestral Jordan River in Canaan far to the west of where he lived. His friend Eliphaz the Temanite dwelt in that area. Job may have travelled widely due to his wealth and reputation.

*"This man was the greatest of all the men of the east."* (Job 1:3f)

"The land of Uz" referred to in the Book of Job occupied the area of 'padan aram' in Mesopotamia where Abram had sojourned before journeying by God's command into the land of Canaan. Its name refers to, Uz, the firstborn son of Aram, the youngest son of Shem, Noah's fifth son. Abram brought Terah his father there; and his brother Nahor and Nahor's wife, Milcah lived there also, likely before Abram later left for Canaan.

Many of the geological observations in the Book of Job would fit into the geographic area Chaldea, the tectonically active region where Abram's progenitors and descendants lived and would have witnessed them. The Book of Job contains the accounts of what his generation personally saw and knew, and also heard by traditions passed on from the older patriarchs, some of whom were born shortly after the Great Flood. There were men older than Job's father still alive at that time.

It is necessary to try and determine approximately how long Job lived and to what general part of the post-Flood era he belonged. That will help explain the accurate firsthand geological and paleontological phenomena witnessed by Job and the earlier patriarchs, and recorded in the Scriptures.

Job's genealogy is not given. His family ties and date of birth remain a mystery. Eliphaz, Bildad, Zophar and Elihu's family connections are all given, but not Job's. To be accepted by the Jewish people as part of the Old Testament canon of Scriptures, Job would have had to have been a descendant of Noah's son, Shem. But that is all we can infer about his origin. A general time frame for Job's life can be established by comparing the Scriptures with one another. Job described himself as an "old man" at the time he lost his wealth, children, health and social stature.

> *"Yea, whereto might the strength of their hands profit me, in whom **old age** was perished?"* (Job 30:2)

Job's three friends provide further evidence that he was an aged man when he suffered his great losses. Normally, a man's friends are his peers and roughly of a similar age. Job, Eliphaz, Bildad and Zophar are described by a young, firsthand witness, Elihu, the son of Barachel the Buzite, of the kindred of Ram, as "very old," had lived a "multitude of years," were "great men," and "aged." (Job 32:6). They had already lived many "Days." Elihu was a young man and the last to speak in Job chapters 32-37.

> *"**Great men** are not always wise, neither do **the aged** understand judgment."* (Job 32:9)

> *"I said, **Days** should speak, and **multitude of years** should teach wisdom."* (Job 32:7)

The age description for these three men, including Job, make them all OLD at the time of the events described in the Book of Job. How old we don't know. Four of the men's ancestries are given, while Job's remains a mystery. Then, "After <u>this</u>," (<u>his suffering</u>) Job lived "one hundred and forty years." Job would have been born among one of the post-flood generations of men like Peleg, Reu, Serug and Terah all of whom lived to ages exceeding 200 years.

> *"After this lived Job **an hundred and forty years**, and saw his sons, and his sons' sons, even four generations. So Job died, being old and full of days."* (Job 42:16-17)

Pastor Jon Harwood corroborated that Job lived another 140 years after he suffered. The writer also asked Rabbi Mark Glickman of Temple B'nai Tikvah in Calgary, who stated that Job lived another 140 years after his trial of suffering ended. So Job and his three friends were "very old" men as stated in Job 32:6.

> *"And Elihu the son of Barachel the Buzite answered and said, I am young, and ye are* ***very old****; wherefore I was afraid, and durst not shew you mine opinion."* (Job 32:6)

Job's father was still alive according to his three friends. They must have met him and known that he was an ancient patriarch. BUT, they also knew there were "very aged" men living who were "much elder than thy (Job's) father." This knowledge suggests that some of the first Post-Flood patriarchs such as Eber and Arphaxad, and even some of the antediluvians such as Noah and his sons could still have been alive at this time. Eliphaz boasts against Job;

> *"What knowest thou, that we know not? What understandest thou, which is not in us? With us are both the gray-headed and very aged men, much elder than thy father."* (Job 15:9, 10)

There were witnesses to the Flood and the Post-Flood 'days of Peleg' still alive during at least part of Job's lifetime. No doubt these men imparted knowledge of the events that had occurred in the past to Eliphaz, Bildad and Zophar; as well as to Job himself. Noah lived for 350 years after the flood, dying in 1998 B.C. while Abram was alive and still living in Chaldea. Noah had seen it all; both before the Flood, and after it had ended.

Elihu the Buzite was a near descendent of Abram's brother, Nahor; Buz being the second eldest son of Nahor's wife, Milcah. Elihu said to Job and his three friends, *"I am young, and ye are very old;"* in Job 32:6. He would have lived on for many years after Job and his friends had passed off the scene. The Book of Job was completed after he died in a manner similar to the gospel record of Jesus' life and ministry in the New Testament. The Holy Spirit moved Elihu to pen the Book of Job, the oldest divinely-inspired book in the Holy Bible. Elihu speaks in the first person tense in Job Chapter 32, showing that he was an active witness and participant in the events being described – and the one who wrote them down by inspiration of the Holy Spirit. He likely wrote it during Abraham's lifetime.

> *"They were amazed, they answered no more: they left off speaking. When I had waited, (for they spake not, but stood still, and answered no more;")* (Job 32:15-16)

Job is estimated to have been, at the very least, between eighty and one hundred years of age to qualify as *"very old"* at the time he suffered. Yes, this is an assumption; but he may have been even older than that. He had already lived long enough to have ten children, *"a very great household,"* eleven thousand 'cattle' and become *"the greatest of all the men of the east."* (Job 1:3) Then he lived almost another century and one-half, *"blessed more than at his beginning,"* having another ten children, twenty-two thousand 'cattle,' and much wealth and favor with his family and acquaintance.

Job's total life span could have been between two hundred and twenty to two hundred and forty years, placing his inferred 'date of birth' within one of the generations of Peleg, Reu, Serug or Nahor based upon the genealogical chart below **(Table 1).** That would make Job a witness of at least a part of the 'days of Peleg' when *"the earth was divided."* These post-flood generations are summarized starting with Shem's son, Arphaxad, who was born two years after the Flood (2349 B.C.). Shem's 3rd son was Arphaxad. Shem's 5th son was Aram; Aram's firstborn son was Uz.

| | |
|---|---|
| Birth of Arphaxad — 2346 B.C. | Age at death — 438 yrs. (1909 B.C.) |
| Birth of Salah — 2312 B.C | Age at death — 438 yrs. (1909 B.C.) |
| Birth of Eber — 2280 B.C. | Age at death — 464 yrs. (1816 B.C.) |
| Birth of Peleg — 2247 B.C.<br>*("the earth was divided")* | Age at death — 239 yrs. (2008 B.C.) |
| Birth of Reu — 2217 B.C. | Age at death — 239 yrs. (1978 B.C.) |
| Birth of Serug — 2185 B.C. | Age at death — 230 yrs. (1935 B.C.) |
| Birth of Nahor — 2155 B.C. | Age of death — 148 yrs. (2007 B.C.) |
| Birth of Terah — 2126 B.C. | Age at death — 205 yrs. (1921 B.C.) |
| Birth of Abraham — 2032 B.C. | Age at death — 175 yrs. (1857 B.C.) |
| Birth of Isaac — 1932 B.C. | Age at death — 180 yrs. (1752 B.C.) |
| Birth of Jacob — 1892 B.C. | Age at death — 147 yrs. (1745 B.C.) |
| Birth of Noah — 2848 B.C. | Age at death — 950 yrs. (1898 B.C.) |

**Table 1:**

Post-Flood genealogy of the patriarchs of the Messianic Line of Shem (based on Usher's dates from the Old Scofield Bible, 1909 A.D.)

# CHAPTER 2

## THE BOOK OF JOB AND CONTINENTAL DRIFT

The Book of Job is older than the other Old Testament Scriptures such as the five Books of Moses, called the Pentateuch. It records descriptions of geological processes that occurred before and during Job's lifetime. It speaks of the entire earth being ruptured and divided, that is, split apart.

**Figures 1,** and **2** (below), compare the secular 'old earth' geological chronology with the Biblical chronology based upon the earth-shaping physical processes described by the patriarch Job, and found also in other books of the Bible. Observation during Biblical human lifetimes of geological processes said to take millions of years by the theory of uniformitarianism casts serious doubt on the entire framework of modern-day, secular evolutionary 'science,' so-called, and the age of the earth derived from it. These findings will be described in the chapters following including genetic evidence from recent studies.

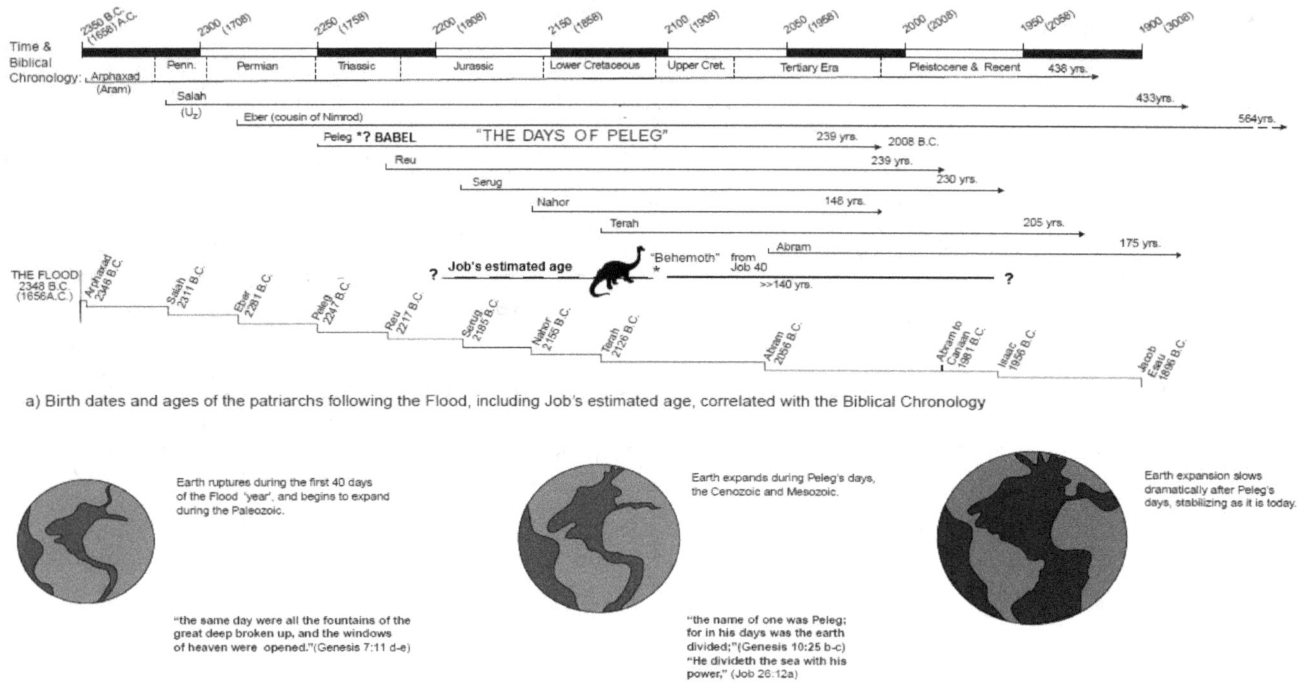


a) Birth dates and ages of the patriarchs following the Flood, including Job's estimated age, correlated with the Biblical Chronology

b)The effects of the expansion of the earth's interior on a pre-Flood granitic crust that originally covered the entire globe. Primordial continents, first outlined by stretching and fragmentation, are separated as they move outward due to the earth's increasing volume. Heavy material from the earth's mantle flows rapidly into the intervening gaps and forms the floors of the growing ocean basins. The initial rupturing and subsequent expansion were essentially completed after three hundred and fifty years — the end of Peleg's day's. Since then the earth has stabilized and near uniform conditions have continued until the present day(modified from Holmes,1965).

**Figure 2**

Break-up of the earth during the "days of Peleg" relating the Biblical chronology to the earth processes of Seafloor Spreading and Continental Drift

Eber's son, Peleg, has one of the most interesting names in the Bible. It means *division*, and is mentioned nearly identically in two books of the Bible; Genesis 10:25

and 1 Chronicles 1:19. By repeating this statement twice in the Scriptures God has given it emphasis for a reason. The Book of Job contains a number of profound scientific statements that are unique to Peleg's generation.

> *"And unto Eber were born two sons: the name of one was Peleg; for in his days was the earth divided; and his brother's name was Joktan." (Genesis 10:25)*

> *"And unto Eber were born two sons: the name of the one was Peleg; because in his days the earth was divided: and his brother's name was Joktan." (1 Chronicles 1:19)*

The Hebrew word for "divided" in this verse is *'palag.'* It means literally, physically torn apart (Ed Frankel; formerly of Calgary Jewish Academy, personal communication). In Peleg's days the whole "earth," not just a locale or a portion, was physically torn apart, including the crust and even deeper portions in the earth's upper mantle. This dividing tore apart the super-continent Pangaea in pieces **(Table 2)**. It was a controlled cataclysm with fragments of continental crust moving apart and new ocean basins opening **(Figure 2)**. This rupture or "dividing" took place roughly between one hundred to three hundred and fifty years following Noah's Flood. That translates to the period between 2246 B.C. and 2007 B.C. In approximately two hundred and forty years the earth's crust was torn asunder and physically divided on a worldwide scale, and was observed by those who lived at that time. The aorist past tense of the verb indicates that the division was essentially completed by the time Peleg died. What caused the earth to be divided? The clue is contained in the Holy Scriptures below.

> *"In the six hundredth year of Noah's life, in the second month, the seventeenth day of the month, <u>the same day were all the fountains of the great deep broken up</u>, and the windows of heaven were opened." (Genesis 7:11)*

Genesis 7:11 and 10:25 together describe the two processes responsible for the earth being divided during the days of Peleg. Total rupturing of the earth at the beginning of the Flood released vast amounts of water from **the great deep**, that is, from within the deeper crust and underlying mantle. The combined effect of fracturing and removal of these subterranean waters was a reduction of pressure and an increase of temperature extending deep into the earth. The highly-pressurized outer core began to break down and convert into mantle material with the consequent release of great heat. The mantle began to expand and develop viscous flowage in convection cells that reached upward to the continental crust. Expansion of the earth and convection in the mantle broke up the rigid, predominantly granitic continental crust and created separate continents and deep ocean basins **(Figures 3 and 6)**. The diameter of the globe increased by approximately 1.7 times its original size. Energy stored within the earth was changed into energy to create seafloor, move continents, raise mountains and deposit tremendous thicknesses of sediment in a short period of time. But it all followed a path obeying the Second Law of Thermodynamics, which is why we see no such processes operating on the same scale today.

a) Reconstructed continents (from Turner and Verhoogen, 1970)

**"And unto Eber were born two sons: the name of one was Peleg; for in his days was the earth divided;"**(Gen.10:25 a-c)

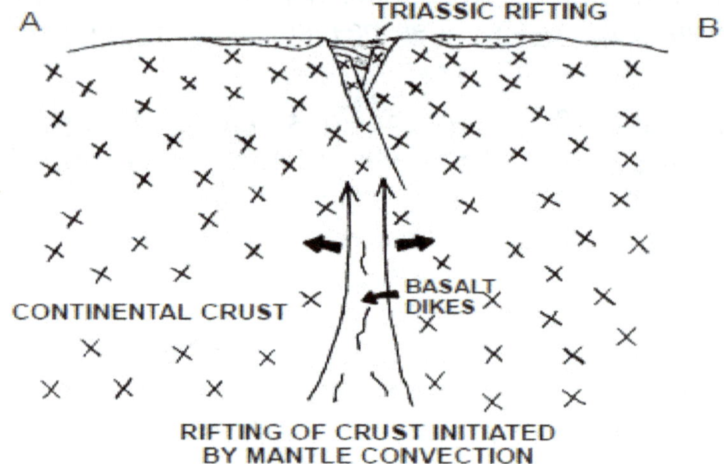


b) Rifting and fragmentation of the granitic continental crust prior to opening

**Figure 3:**

Dividing of the earth during the "days of Peleg" involved the rupturing of continental crust and the fragmentation of the supercontinent Pangaea.

The Bible is telling us that the earth has expanded and its density has decreased since creation. These statements in Genesis are consistent with twentieth century scientific discoveries related to plate tectonics and continental drift. Only in the twentieth century did scientists begin to postulate, and later understand, that the earth's crust had been literally *"divided"* on a worldwide scale. One of the first scientists to offer a credible explanation was Alfred Wegener in 1910.

Earlier workers had expressed the belief that continents had been torn apart and separated on a gigantic scale but Wegener provided the most conclusive evidence in his suite of maps portraying different geologic 'time' periods. Today, the timing of the dividing of the earth (Pangaea) is better understood and accepted by the scientific community as a whole. The entire breakup described in **Table 2** (below) did not require 245 million years but only about 250 years (See **Figure 1**). **Table 2** shows the history of the breakup of Pangaea.

| MAJOR BREAKUP EVENT | GEOLOGICAL PERIOD | OTHER EVENTS |
|---|---|---|
| 1. Africa/Asia connection | Tertiary (Miocene) | Western Tethys Sea isolated |
| 2. Drake Passage opened (S. America & Antarctica) | Tertiary (Oligocene) | |
| 3. Collison of India with Eurasia | Tertiary (Eocene) | Himalaya Mts. begin to form |
| 4. Opening of North Atlantic | Tertiary (Lower Eocene) | Aborted Labrador Rift |
| 5. Separation of Greenland & Europe | Tertiary (Lower Eocene) | |
| 6. Separation of Australia & Antarctica | Upper Cretaceous (Campanian) | |
| 7. Separation of North America & Greenland | Upper Cretaceous (Campanian) | Highest relative sea level |
| 8. Separation of India & Madagascar | Upper Cretaceous (Santonian) | Rising sea level |

| | | |
|---|---|---|
| 9. Rapid separation of Africa & S. America: high rate of seafloor spreading | Upper Cretaceous (Cenomanian) | Central & S. Atlantic connected; high sea level; extensive volcanism |
| 10. Breakup of W. Gondwana: Separation of | Lower Cretaceous (Barremian) | Opening of Arctic, South Atlantic & Indian Oceans |
| Africa & S. America + Breakup of E. Gondwana: | | |
| Separation of Australia-Antarctica & India-Madag. | | |
| 11. Breakup of E. & W. Gondwana: Separation of | Upper Jurassic (Tithonian) | Formation of Somali Basin along northeast Gondwana |
| Africa & Madagascar-India | | |
| 12. Separation of North America & Africa | Middle Jurassic (Bathonian) | Opening of Central Atlantic Ocean: rapid rise sea level |
| 13. Extensive rift valley system formed across | Upper Triassic - Lower Jurassic | Stage set for formation of Central Atlantic; beginning |
| Northwestern Gondwana | | of progressive rise of sea level |
| 14. Breakup of Gondwana begins: Separation of China/Indochina from E. Gondwana | Upper Permian | Gondwana drifting northward |

**Table 2**

The secular geological history of the breakup of Pangaea that occurred during the Biblical days of Peleg between approximately 2250 B.C. and 2000 B.C. (See **Figures 1, 2** and **5**)

> "Wegener's highly ingenious concept of the evolution of the continents and their distribution is graphically illustrated by his own maps, strange and fantastic on first acquaintance, but now widely familiar. For this combination of Laurasia and Gondwanaland, making up the whole land area of the globe, Wegener proposed the name **Pangaea** (Greek for 'all earth'). The present distribution of the continents was regarded as a result of fragmentation of Pangaea by rifting, followed by a drifting apart of the individual masses." (Holmes, A., 1964, Principles of Physical Geology, pp. 1200-01)

Arthur Holmes, one of the twentieth century's most brilliant geologists, wrote that continental drift was best explained by an expanding earth and mantle convection. His theoretical assertion concerning the evolution of the earth is in agreement with Scripture. The significant difference is that modern 'science' teaches that the latest phase of spreading occurred over two hundred and forty-five million years, beginning in the Late Permian and continuing to the present. God's Word specifies rapid displacements occurring between the Flood 'year' and the end of Peleg's lifetime - "the days of Peleg" - a period of about three and one-half centuries. Since that time the earth reached its near present diameter and all physical geological processes have since slowed dramatically to a now near-uniform state by a process of diastrophic or orogenic entropy. Lyell based his uniformitarian doctrine upon this static end state. It was patently wrong; and so was Darwin for following Lyell in formulating his theory of evolution. We shall now examine several branches of geology to show that "the present is NOT the key to the past" in light of this knowledge and the Biblical chronology.

# CHAPTER 3

## THE BOOK OF JOB AND SEAFLOOR SPREADING

Catastrophic events are consistent with the geology of the area in which Job lived. The Land of Uz was near the southern coastline of the Tethys Sea where both rifting and colliding of crustal plates occurred **(Figure 4).** The region surrounding Job's homeland was very dynamic from a plate tectonic perspective and his words describing these processes are scientifically understandable. Job's speech does not use modern technical terms or name the geographic entities involved, but he speaks in manner that parallels modern science's description of continental drift and seafloor spreading.

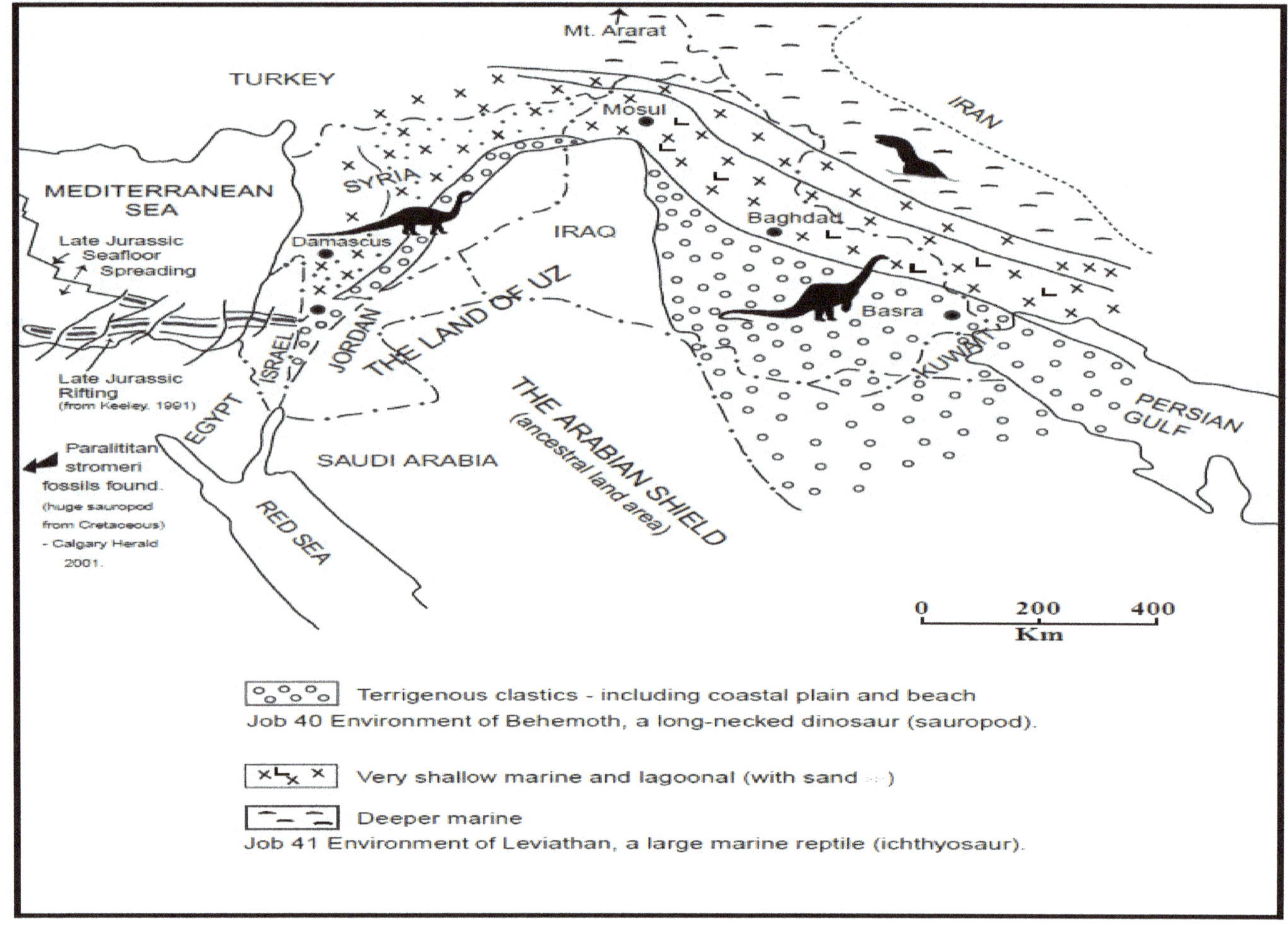


**Figure 4:**

Secular paleogeographic map of the Early Cretaceous Berriasian ('140 my' before present) to Aptian ('112 my' before present) in relation to the Biblical "behemoth" dinosaur and the "leviathan" mosasaur or ichthyosaur described in Job Chapters 40 and 41 (modified from Buday, T., 1980, The Regional Geology of Iraq)

Job lived during the time of Peleg and saw "**the earth divided**." He witnessed portions of Pangaea, the large landmass accreted during and after 'Noah's' Flood, break apart, and oceans open through the mechanism of seafloor spreading. The following Scriptures describe this process.

> *"Who hath divided a watercourse for the overflowing of waters, or a way for the lightning of thunder;"* (Job 38:25)
>
> *"Or who shut up the sea with doors, when it brake forth, as if it had issued out of the womb? And brake up for it my decreed place, and set bars and doors,"* (Job 38:8, 10)
>
> *Thou didst divide the sea by thy strength: thou brakest the heads of the dragons in the waters."* (Psalm 74:13)

The Bible mentions seas forming in the manner known to modern earth scientists. Job knew that oceans opened in a visible dynamic way by the breaking up of continental crust. In the above verses, the word *"divided"* means physically split asunder, the same usage as in the earlier reference to Peleg's days. They describe the fragmentation of the earth's crust and the opening of *"the sea"* or *"a watercourse."* It involved the breakup of a continent, or a portion thereof. For how could a body of water have opened unless two fragments of crust first drifted apart? Job 38:8 & 10 describe crustal rifting and then inundation by sea waters along the intervening faulted depression **(Figure 3)**. *"Brake forth...out of the womb"* indicates that this process occurred rapidly and with catastrophic flooding. Job lived on the Arabian Platform near the ancestral Mediterranean Sea, the Tethys, where rifting and seafloor spreading took place during the Cenozoic and Mesozoic eras. No living human being in today's world sees such events, for they have ended.

> "It would appear that quite suddenly, early in the Bathonian (Middle Jurassic) the rift was able to propagate westwards across the entire Egyptian offshore. As in eastern Egypt earlier, on the margins of the rift, crustal thinning led to fault block rotation and partial collapse of the crust." (Keeley, M., 1991, The Jurassic System in Northern Egypt, Journal of Petroleum Geology, pp. 49-64)

Their plate tectonic diagram for the Late Jurassic shows the Land of Uz bordering a zone of extensive faulting and separation as the sea opened and the rift propagated eastward **(Figure 4)**. Another example, the Red Sea, formed during the Tertiary Period when the Arabian Peninsula broke away from the African continental plate. As the two halves drifted apart waters from the Indian Ocean flooded into the faulted depression. The Mediterranean was a shallow, salt-floored basin later flooded by the breaching of a barrier along the Strait of Gibraltar. Scripture describes events such as these from the same area as Job lived in non-technical terms.

Modern science understandably explains plate tectonics in more detail than the Bible because of the use of recent technology and terminology. The break-up of Gondwana formed three oceans and four continental fragments. One giant rupture created the Atlantic Ocean, with Africa and Western Europe, and the Americas on opposing sides. These new continents drifted away from the Mid-Atlantic Ridge, a linear submarine mountain range composed of upwelling basaltic lava. This spreading center formed a new ocean basin over four thousand miles in width. Accurate global mapping in the last century permitted the fitting together of these and other continental fragments using their modern shelf edges. It resulted in the reconstruction of the single continent Pangaea that existed before the earth was divided in Peleg's days.

**Below are recent geology textbook excerpts pertinent to seafloor spreading and continental drift. Note the close correspondence between Scripture and the accompanying secular scientific description.**

> *"And unto Eber were born two sons: the name of one was Peleg; for in his days was the earth divided;"* (Genesis 10:25a-c and 1 Chronicles 1:19a-c)
>
> *"He divideth the sea with his power, and by his understanding he smiteth through the proud."* (Job 26:12)
>
> "A striking picture of what may be happening has recently been presented by Morgan and Le Pichon. Both these authors assume that an outer shell of the earth can be divided into a small number of rigid blocks that move more or less independently as they are rafted along; these blocks are jostled about much as gigantic ice floes. Where two blocks move apart, an ocean ridge forms and new crust is produced (i.e., a new ocean basin); where two blocks move toward each other, either shortening and compression produce a fold mountain belt, or crust is destroyed as one block is thrust under the other. The hypothesis of continuous creation of oceanic crust accounts for the small thickness of sediments on the ocean floor (which) are continuously carried away by the moving crust which has been aptly described as a "conveyor belt with a built-in magnetic tape recorder." (Turner, F., et al, 1970, The Earth: An Introduction to Physical Geology, pp. 683-690)

These two descriptions are separated by nearly four thousand years of time yet are saying the same thing. Scripture is that of an eyewitness accurately describing the 'evolution' of our modern continents and oceans within a Biblical chronology. Secular science uses global mapping and sophisticated geophysical instruments to decipher seafloor spreading and continental drift within an uniformitarian context. Although Job did not know that mantle convection and basaltic upwelling from the earth's lower crust caused new seafloor to form, he did see its physical surface expression. His generation witnessed oceans and seas open, close and then dry up. They also saw mighty rivers form and later dry up and disappear. The geological record contains many examples of ancient rivers whose eroded channels and sedimentary deposits now lie buried deep beneath the earth's surface. Examples occur in almost all of the geologic periods. The Cretaceous of Alberta contains buried valleys within which large rivers flowed during the times of Peleg and Job. They were then abandoned and buried under younger deposits of sediments. A short life cycle for major rivers is not characteristic of today, but it must have happened often in the immediate Post-Flood world, as recorded in the Bible.

Instead of occurring over millions of years these events took place during men's lifetimes (see **Figure 2** and **Table 1**). That is why the Scriptural accounts so accurately portray geological processes.

> *"Behold, he withholdeth the waters, and they dry up: also he sendeth them out, and they overturn the earth."* (Job 12:15)

> *"Thou didst cleave the fountain and the flood: thou driedst up mighty rivers."* (Psalm 74:15)

How long did it take to form our modern oceans? Today, seafloor spreading occurs at minute rates, about 2 ½ cm/yr. in the Atlantic and up to 9 cm/yr. near the East Pacific Rise. But the Bible says that these oceans formed during Peleg's days! Twice the Scriptures say, *"in his days was the earth divided."* This process involved the complete cleaving open and splitting apart of Pangaea **(Figure 5)**. The verb tense *"was divided"* indicates a past action essentially completed *"in his days,"* a time span of approximately two hundred and forty years! Therefore, during Peleg's lifetime the Central Atlantic Ocean between the U.S.A and northwest Africa spread to almost its present width of about four thousand miles. The South Atlantic opened fifty to one hundred years later and developed to its present minimum extent of about two thousand miles. Using Biblical chronology, these distances translate to average spreading rates of between seventeen to twenty miles per year, and are consistent with the testimony of Scripture. The rates of spreading no doubt varied in time. High spreading rates translated into rising sea levels on the continents, and slower spreading rates with dropping water levels, all other factors being equal. In the Alberta Basin, Cretaceous sedimentary rocks contain rich dinosaur bone beds. Many of these great creatures lived on coastal plains near inflowing rivers and the sea. A surge of waters due to high sea floor spreading rates in the Late Cretaceous coupled with rapid subsidence along the ancestral Rocky Mountain front to the west would lead to flooding of estuaries and low lying parts of the coastal plain drowning these big animals in large numbers. Geological processes as well as other factors led to their extinction.

> *"Thou didst divide the sea by thy strength: thou brakest the heads of the dragons in the waters."* (Psalm 74:13)

Men watched shorelines recede out of sight in less than a decade. Movement was many orders of magnitude greater than that postulated by modern science. The earth, having been ruptured and weakened during the Great Flood, when "all the fountains of the great deep were broken up," was now rapidly expanding in size, dividing the earth's continental crust into spreading and colliding fragments. So rapid was this spreading that some of the colliding crustal blocks were thrust down into the earth's mantle and may have been caught up in the convection currents there and carried deeper into the earth. This phenomenon could have taken place anytime between Noah's Flood and the end of the "days of Peleg." Dr. Marcus Ross, a PhD geologist and university professor, stated the following:

> "Modern NASA seismologists have discovered that there are indeed huge, cool slabs of rock under North America down near the core of the earth itself, in areas that should have warmed up if millions of years of time were what brought those cool slabs of rock down into the mantle." (Ross, M., 2014, Evolution's Achilles' Heels)

Magnetic N-S pole reversals in the Atlantic Ocean seafloor correlate to the dividing of the earth in the Biblical chronology. Normal and reverse polarity magnetic stripes mirror opposite sides of the Mid-Atlantic Ridge, and are approximately comparable in number (270) to the time period in years ($250^{+}$) comprising "Peleg's days," spanning the secular Early Triassic to Middle Miocene portion of the geological column **(Figures 5 and 6)**. Reversals in the earth's magnetic field occurred rapidly, were of short duration constrained by the length of Peleg's lifetime. Physical rupture and rapid expansion of the earth, beginning with Noah's Flood and concluding at the end of "the days of Peleg," involved electrochemical and phase changes between the inner core and mantle. The magnetic couplets seem to correlate to short time intervals, possibly annuals. They look like varve couplets that record generally 'annual' summer-winter, rapid and slow depositional cycles in glacial lakes. Could the magnetic pole reversals be caused by fluctuating rates of mantle convection tied in with the earth's annual orbit around the sun? The position of the earth and sun also seem to influence the 'half-lives' of some radioactive isotopes, notably $Si^{32}$, $R^{226}$, $Cs^{137}$ and $Co^{60}$ (Mason, J., 2014, Evolution's Achilles' Heels). Evidence for rapid reversals of the earth's magnetic field were recently corroborated by 'old earth' geologists studying young volcanic rocks in the Pacific Northwest.

> "They were looking at lava flows that would only take a couple of weeks in order to form. They took measurements of the skin of the lava to see the magnetic orientation. They were expecting to see no change as they went deeper into the lava where the interior should shift only slightly. Then they found that the outside skin of the lava pointed north, and the inside pointed south. So we have confirming evidence that switches in the magnetic field has to happen rapidly, which is exactly what Flood geologists expect." (Ross, M., 2014, Evolution's Achilles' Heels)

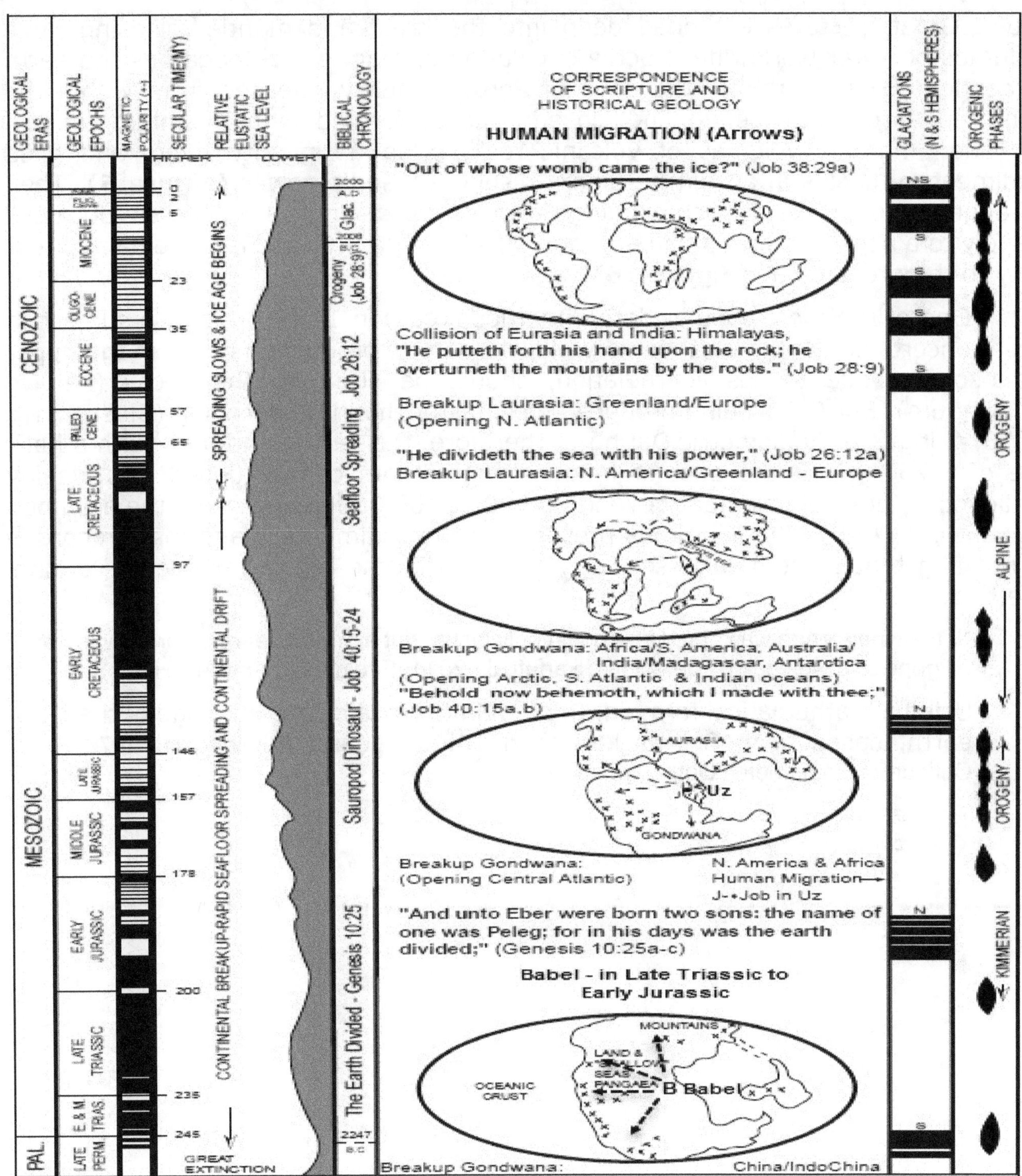


**Figure 5**

The Biblical chronology of Peleg's days compared to Cenozoic and Mesozoic geological phenomena and their uniformitarian geological interpretation. (modified from Shell Oil Company, 1990)

God broke up *"all the fountains of the great deep"* during Noah's Flood, and then stopped them (Genesis 8:2), preventing the complete destruction of the earth's crust. Great fractures extended deep into the crust and mantle releasing huge volumes of water worldwide. Ductile circulation of mantle rock began as the earth expanded. By the end of "the days of Peleg," energy released from within the ruptured earth had opened and closed oceans, formed high mountain ranges, extruded massive volumes of volcanic rock, dried up mighty rivers and filled sedimentary basins in an extraordinary display of God's power **(Figure 5)**. Then through entropy, like a clock winding down, these geological processes 'decayed' rapidly to a near static condition around 2000-to-1900 B.C. and have remained that way to the present day **(Figure 16)**.

One of the most popular dating methods, carbon 14 ($C^{14}$), is also subject to great uncertainty. If the earth is very old, the rate of production of $C^{14}$ in the upper atmosphere, due to cosmic radiation, should be equal to the decay (i.e., in equilibrium). But $C^{14}$ is being produced 24% faster than it is decaying (Slusher, H., 1973, Critique of Radiometric Dating). Therefore, the earth is not old. With a half-life of 5,760 years, the best of modern instruments cannot detect this weakly radioactive, unstable element beyond 80,000 to 100,000 years, given the assumed current decay rate. Its ubiquitous presence in the sedimentary and fossil record is a red flag that something is seriously wrong with the entire radioactive 'dating' method.

> "If the whole earth was pure $C^{14}$ it could only last about a million years before it was all gone and we couldn't detect it." (Sarfati, J., 2014, Evolution's Achilles' Heels)
>
> Using a mathematical formula, Dr. Melvin Cook calculated the age of the earth, based upon $C^{14}$, as less than 10,000 years. (Slusher, H., 1973, Critique of Radiometric Dating, pp. 37-40)

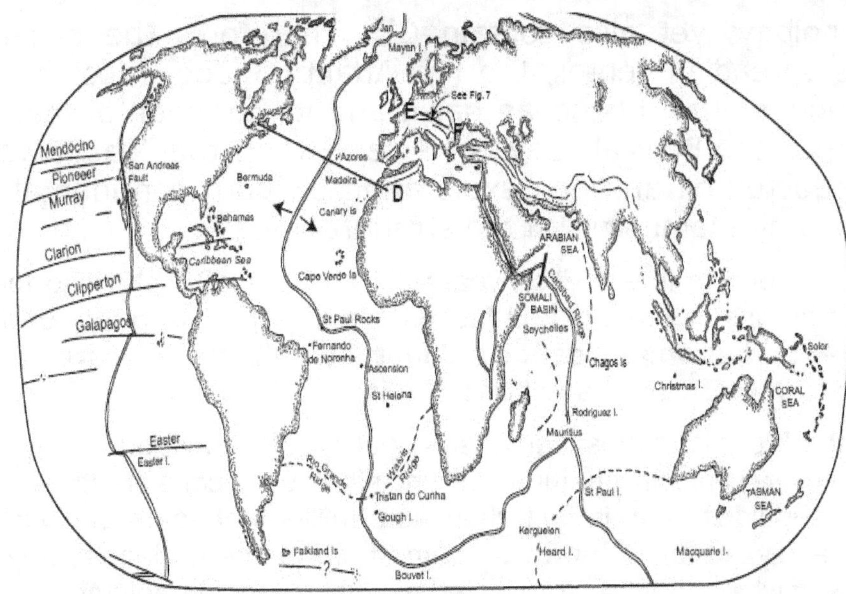


a) Present distribution of the oceans and continents complete at the end of Peleg's days (from Longwell and Flint, 1965).

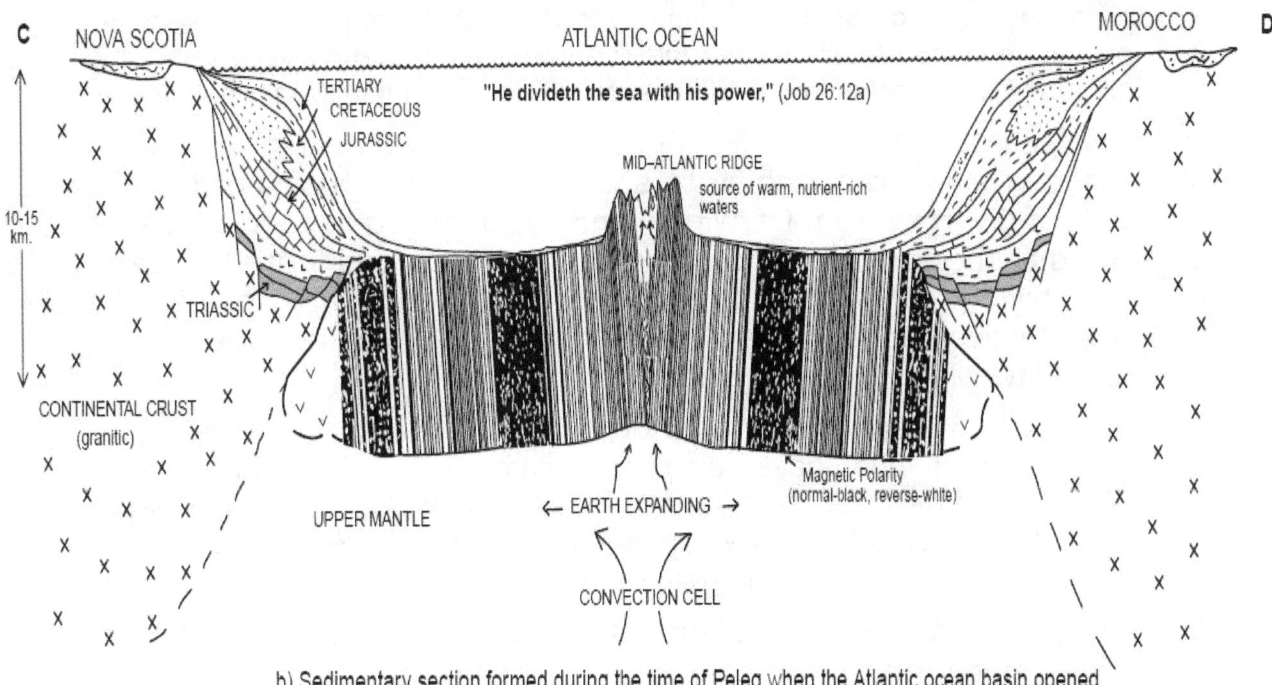


b) Sedimentary section formed during the time of Peleg when the Atlantic ocean basin opened.

**Figure 6**

Seafloor Spreading and Continental Drift – the end result of "the earth divided" during the "days of Peleg"

Recently, scientists have been discovering carbon-14 in rocks, minerals and materials that are supposedly millions or billions of years old by radioactive dating methods. These include diamonds that were injected through many kilometers of Precambrian continental crust from the earth's mantle. The thick sedimentary rocks of the Triassic through Tertiary on opposing margins of the central Atlantic Ocean contain fossils and coals that are supposedly up to 245 millions of years old based upon geochronology, yet also contain $C^{14}$. Therefore, the basaltic ocean crust forming at the spreading center, the Mid-Atlantic Ridge, must be young along its entire length and width. This ocean basin and its continental margin sedimentary rocks correlate to the Biblical "days of Peleg" when the "earth was divided." The writer has conducted oil and gas exploration on both continental margins in this diagram, making him familiar with the stratigraphy.

> "In diamonds one to three billion years old....we find $C^{14}$ showing they can't be millions or billions of years old. In fact, **$C^{14}$ is a very strong ally of the Biblical time scale, and strong evidence against the millions of years of evolution.**" (Sarfati, J., 2014, Evolution's Achilles' Heels)

> "$C^{14}$ dating of fossils of mosasaurs, sea shells, petrified wood or any of the fossil fuels, especially coal, oil or natural gas since the 1970s consistently shows us ages that there shouldn't be if, in fact, they were millions of years old. When creation scientists analyzed for $C^{14}$ in coal seams from different places, they found that regardless of where they were collected or what layers of geology they were found in, ALL samples registered statistically the same amount of carbon 14. Rather than providing evidence of gradual deposition over 10s or 100s of millions of years – the identical amounts of $C^{14}$ in all of the coal samples actually shows that they were all buried in the recent past." (Ross, M., 2014, Evolution's Achilles' Heels, 2014)

Many lines of evidence combine to show that the earth cannot be 'old age.' Secular science, if divorced from Darwinian and Lyellian ideology, dovetails with the Bible, showing that the earth and the processes which shaped it are thousands and not millions or billions of years old! It is profoundly saddening to see the bias expressed by some evolutionary scientists concerning the evolution-creation debate. It seems like brainwashing has occurred.

> "We take the side of science in spite of the patent absurdity of some of its constructs...because we have a prior commitment, a commitment to materialism...Moreover, that materialism is absolute, for we cannot allow a Divine Foot in the door." (Evolution's Achilles' Heels, 2014, quoting Professor R. Lewontin, Evolutionary biologist, Harvard University)

Quoted below is an example of one of the absurdities that Lewontin alludes to, and there are many, many more.

> "Let this process go on for millions on millions of years, each year, on millions of individuals of many kinds and it would produce a perfect eye by Natural Selection. (Darwin, C., 1859, On the Origin of Species, p. 81)

Darwin added that his theory would break down if millions upon millions of years were not available for the eye to evolve by in this manner. The eye could never evolve in any manner in any amount of time.

He also stated that he looked forward in the future to the creation – evolution controversy being debated and settled by impartial (fair, unprejudiced, unbiased) scientific arguments.

> "I look forward with confidence to the future, to young and rising naturalists, who will be able to view both sides of the question with impartiality." (Ibid, p. 207)

Followers of Darwinian evolution have moved far from their founder's hopes by using suppression, coercion and intimidation to marginalize, exclude and silence creation teachers and scientists from having their research and voices heard in the academic community. Darwin did not advocate excluding independent creation from the discussion of origins, or of teaching them. He felt his theory of evolution would destroy the creation theology by force of persuasion, not by force of repression. Today's suppression of creation science is wrong and damaging to students and teachers alike in our schools, colleges and universities. In Alberta, Creation science is scorned by evolutionists as pseudo-science conducted by pseudo-scientists according to Harry Nibourg of Big Valley Creation Science Museum (personal communication).

> "In the U.S. there is no freedom to teach the biblical account of Creation in the public schools. It is against the law! Evolution has had a total monopoly on education for decades. **Evolution is the official religion of our schools.** It took only one man, Charles Darwin, to outlaw the Bible and Christianity and corrupt our schools." (Helton, D., 2021, Evolution: Another False Religion of Humanism, pp. 42-43)

This writer encourages the reader to keep an open mind as he or she reads on through the following chapters. Both Biblical and secular evidence are used to support a young earth.

# CHAPTER 4

## THE BOOK OF JOB AND MOUNTAIN BUILDING

Structural geology is a branch of study dealing with the deformation of the earth's crust by orogenic or mountain-building forces, supposedly acting slowly over long periods of time. The Rocky Mountains west of Calgary, and the Alps of southern Europe are considered to be 'young' mountains, having formed in the Laramide and Alpine orogenies about 40 to 50 million years ago according to uniformitarian geologists. They comprise long linear belts of folded and faulted rocks that are structurally complex.

Mountain building or orogeny is a natural product of seafloor spreading and continental drift. As crustal plates collided, compression and folding of thick sedimentary layers created mountains along convergent boundaries. Volcanism accompanied an orogeny where oceanic crust was overridden and slid beneath a 'granitic' continent by a process called subduction. Volcanic mountains can form in the areas of subduction. Many mountain belts contain very complex types of folded structures. The Canadian Rockies and Foothills display stacked layers of thrust-faulted and folded Paleozoic carbonates and Mesozoic clastics (front cover and **Figure 8**). The most complex folds are called nappes. These recumbent or overturned fold belts developed when the deep crust swelled upward causing the overlying sedimentary layers to flow downslope like viscous plastic. Under the influence of gravity, they wrapped one over another in stacks of faulted and folded sheets called nappes. These complex folds were later eroded to form spectacular mountains. The European Alps are a prime example and have undergone extreme deformation in some regions as the following accounts demonstrate.

> "Under extreme deformation some folds have been completely overturned. *A fold of which the axial plane is essentially horizontal is a **recumbent fold.*** ...In this fold the layers in one limb are upside down. Huge recumbent folds are common in the Alps and some other mountain belts." (Longwell, C., and Flint R., 1965, Introduction to Physical Geology, p. 360)

> "The resulting structure is almost incredibly complex, and even after generations of field study some of it is not fully understood. ...folding and faulting began at an early stage and the resulting uplifts made chains of islands dividing the geosyncline into several troughs in which sedimentary deposits built up continuously. Under compressive stress, the rising masses under the island chains were moved together and finally piled up, one above another. Argand's diagrams emphasize the development of immense recumbent folds, a conspicuous feature of Alpine structure, but to avoid confusion these diagrams omit the large thrust faults by which the folds were sliced and moved northward. (Ibid, p. 425)

Scientists have measured current horizontal and vertical earth movements around the world and extrapolated these values to explain orogenic deformation in the context of vast ages of geologic time. They have used radiometric age dating to support their theories of mountain building. John Shelton, an uniformitarian geologist, wrote the following concerning their rates:

> "The examples cited above indicate that deformation rates of from 1 to 5 feet per century are a plausible measure of the speed of diastrophic events in active areas during modern times...so far as we can tell deformation need never have taken place any more rapidly than it is taking place right now in the more active parts of the continents." (Shelton, J., 1966, Geology Illustrated, pp. 417-418)

But is the present *really* the key to the past? The Bible describes complex tectonic deformation of the earth's crust in a completely different time frame than uniformitarian geologists. It identifies natural processes in so simple and sublime a manner that they can be easily missed.

Job spoke about tectonic deformation with the understanding and accuracy of an experienced structural geologist. The verse below states in a few words a geological process that was unknown to man until the middle of the nineteenth century, and only then after many, many years of measurements by structural geologists in the Alpine Mountains of Europe **(Figure 7a)**.

> *"He putteth forth his hand upon the rock; he overturneth the mountains by the roots. He cutteth out rivers among the rocks and his eye seeth every precious thing."* (Job 28:9-10)

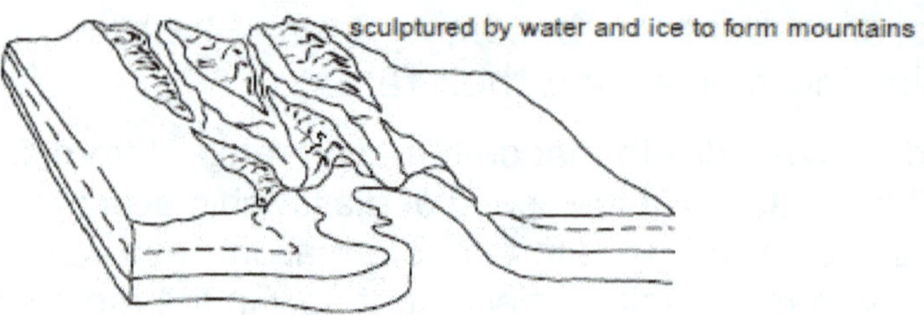


III) Erosion of recumbent fold.

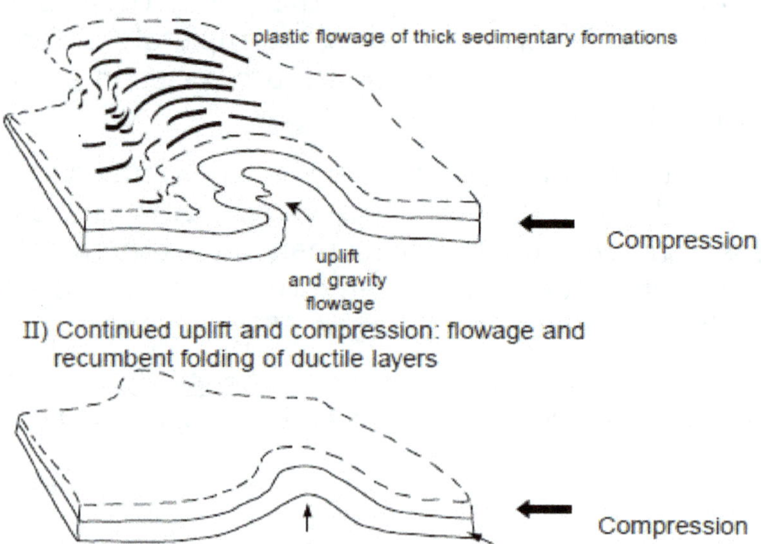


I) Compression and uplift from the 'roots' of the future mountains

a) Job describes complex mountains being overturned 'by the roots.'

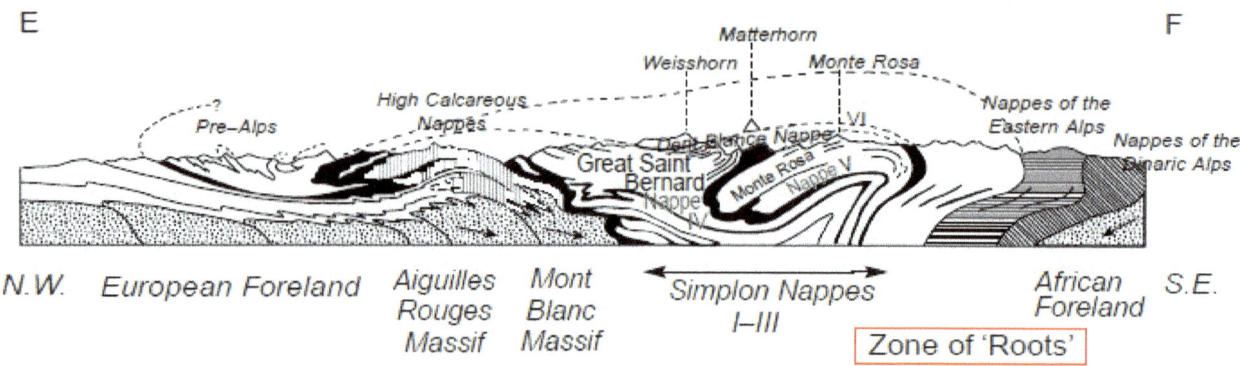


b)Tectonic section across The Western Alps based on the idea that the great recumbent folds were driven from the Tethys geosyncline and its basement by the vice–like approach of The African and European forelands. (from: Holmes, 1965)

**Figure 7**

Alpine-style mountain building described in the Book of Job.

By mentioning that mountains have **roots**, he revealed scientific facts far beyond his time. The continental crust is thicker under mountain belts, with the isostatic load of the rock mass producing a downward bulge that can be measured by gravity meters. By using the word "settled" the Scriptures refer to mountains "sinking down gradually under their own weight," forming the mountain's root. (Winston College Dictionary, 1946)

> *"Before the mountains were settled, before the hills was I brought forth:"* (Proverbs 8:25)

Structural geologists first discovered the Alpine 'Zone of Roots' in the nineteenth century A.D. **(Figure 7)**. Weak zones in the crust extruded volcanic lavas that pierced through the sedimentary deposits. The 'Root Zone' or core of many orogenic belts flowed in a manner similar to glaciers **(Figure 7b)**. Such highly-deformed metamorphic rocks extend from Morocco, through southern Europe into Turkey, across Iraq and Iran, and into India and Nepal. Strata of a similar age were uplifted and folded in the Western Cordillera of North America. Yet Job described a mountain system developing from a root, meaning rocks that are deeply buried in the earth's crust are uplifted, complexly folded, and then exhumed and exposed by erosion into their deepest core rocks. The rising root caused the shallower sedimentary layers to swell upward and flow laterally like pancake batter down an inclined surface, sometimes into the sea. The resulting faulted and overturned sedimentary layers many thousands of feet thick comprise the giant nappes that are now eroded into some of the most beautiful mountain ranges in the world. Examples occur in Italy, Turkey and southern Iran. A dynamic picture of orogenic uplift and deformation is described in Scripture. It, and Job 28:9 (above), define the complex processes involved in an orogeny or mountain building event.

> *"GOD is our refuge and strength, a very present help in trouble. Therefore will not we fear, though the earth be removed, and though the mountains be carried into the midst of the sea; Though the waters thereof roar and be troubled, though the mountains shake with the swelling thereof. Selah."* (Psalm 46:1-3)

The preceding verses illustrate the natural human response to earth upheavals of the magnitude of those mentioned in the Book of Job, initial fear accompanied by a flight to God for safety. Obviously, such enormous uplift would be observed as swelling of the earth's crust from a great distance away and it would be frightening to behold. Strong earthquakes, volcanism and dramatic erosion would have accompanied the building of mountains. The divinely inspired Scriptures correctly speak of these orogenic processes as catastrophic events within human history.

Arthur Holmes, one of the Twentieth Century's greatest geologists, illustrated the Alpine "Zone of Roots" in his classic geology textbook, *"The Principles of Physical Geology."* **(Figure 7b)** He also wrote extensively about the tremendous uplift and deformation associated with its development.

> "Along this zone tectonic subsidence and subsequent uplift reached their maximum amplitude, so that today in the Ticino valleys we can see the swirling flow structures

> of (metamorphic) migmatites formed from schists that were originally Triassic sediments. Evidently the latter were highly mobilized not only by heat, but also by the introduction of hot lubricating emanations. Whereas the transport of the Helvetian nappes appears to have been by superficial gravity gliding, that of the Pennine nappes required deep-seated flowage, which, as we shall see, may also have been activated by gravity." (Holmes, A., 1964, Principles of Physical Geology, p. 1161)

How have mountains grown through time? Uniformitarian geologists teach that orogenic systems took many millions of years to form and then were deeply eroded, sometimes down to their roots. The Bible also describes the processes of mountain building and subsequent destruction or erosion but in a completely different context. There are many examples of 'old' mountains such as the Urals of Russia, the Appalachians of the eastern United States and the Caledonides of Scotland. They formed during the Flood 'year' and in the century following. The dividing of the earth during Peleg's days produced the world-girdling belt of 'young,' mountains such as the Andes, Alps and Himalayas. The Word of God describes orogenic movements within a Biblical chronology where rising masses of semi-consolidated sediment underwent plastic flowage, folding and faulting, subsequent erosion and re-deposition as new basin filling. The whole process is attributed to God's **"anger"** and judgment of sin that is always of short duration but intense beyond human comprehension.

> *"Which removeth the mountains, and they know not: which overturneth them in his anger."* (Job 9:5)

Verse five describes both the removal *and* overturning of mountains. The colon gives the two halves of the verse equal weight, stating that the mountains were eroded to form new layers of thick sediment that were again overturned and folded. The omnipotent God is the active mover. He *"removeth the mountains,"* signifies the active uplift, erosion and destruction of a very great mass of rock in relation to the overfolding processes described above. Rapid physical displacement of great rock masses through gravity sliding suggests people actually saw these mountains removed. The phrase *"and they know not:"* indicates they were 'taken away' within a very short time and 'disappeared,' only to be rebuilt again in the same fashion – by God's power. Sentence construction is precise scientifically in the Scriptures.

The Alps were eroded and rebuilt as the African and European continental plates continued to collide. Geologists discovered that marine basins in front of the nappes were filled with sediments eroded from these folds and then were subsequently deformed as the orogeny progressed northward. This is the reason why the Alpine mountain ranges contain generally younger sediments and folding toward the north. Their deformed strata show plastic flowage and horizontal displacements extending many tens of kilometers from where the sediments were originally deposited. The beds seem to have melted and flowed like wax in intricate convoluted fold patterns. This means that they could not have been fully lithified or solidified by burial over a long period of time. Sedimentation, burial and uplift of the ductile or plastic formations occurred over a short time in recent earth history. Otherwise the formations would have hardened into brittle rock. **Figure 8** shows examples of tight folding in hard, brittle carbonate rocks from the Canadian Rockies in Alberta. These mountains formed in the latter part of the "days of Peleg," called the Cenozoic in secular geology. In the early Tertiary era, Paleozoic carbonates were thrust-faulted over younger Cretaceous sandstones and shales that contain rich dinosaur fossil beds to the east near Drumheller, Alberta, two hundred kilometers to the east. Note how the tightly folded, hard brittle limestones show little evidence of fracturing because they were deformed in a soft, ductile state shortly after being deposited about 4500 years ago.

> *"The hills melted like wax at the presence of the LORD, at the presence of the Lord of the whole earth."* (Psalm 97:5)
>
> "There are some things about modern mountain belts that we see that don't seem to fit with this conventional view (of millions of years for mountain building). Rock is brittle. It doesn't bend very easily: if you bend it; it breaks. On a big scale you might be able to get some big bends out of a large rock; but these bends are tight and close, and you can walk from one end of them to the other. This type of bending and folding without breaking brittle rock means that maybe it wasn't brittle rock at the time of its formation. There might have been much softer materials; after all they were laid down during Noah's Flood. They've been compacted down, started off horizontal; but then as tectonic movements occurred, it shifted and folded them while they were still soft. So when we look at it this way we realize that the tall mountain chains – the Alps, the Rockies, the Himalayas, etc. – they didn't exist before the Flood. The whole reason they exist is because of the Flood." (Ross, M., 2014, Evolution's Achilles' Heels, Creation Science International)

**Figure 8**

Mt. Kidd (top), 2,958 m in the Kananaskis Range, Alberta – at north end of 450 km. long Lewis Thrust Fault; and Mt. Cascade (bottom), 2998 m in the Vermillion Range, Banff, Alberta – both mountains are in thick, folded Paleozoic carbonate and shale of the Canadian Rockies

Secular geology says that the Laramide orogeny formed the Rocky Mountains starting 70 to 80 million years ago and ending 35-55 million years ago in the early

Tertiary. Yet, Biblical chronology (Job 28:9 and 14: 11) says that Post-Paleozoic orogeny and deposition were largely completed by the end of Peleg's days about 4000 years ago. Sediments were deposited and uplifted so rapidly that they did not have time to fully harden or lithify. Folding occurred when these strata were still ductile and capable of deforming in the plastic state.

Dr. Ray Price, former Director of the Geological Survey of Canada is an outstanding scientist who has mapped large areas of the Rocky Mountains. He stated that mountain building must be considered in view of plastic deformation of rock that behaved like a ductile or viscous fluid. Dr. Andrew Bally supported his conclusions at the Geocanada 2000 Meeting in Calgary. Together they concurred as follows:

> "We need to look at ductile (plastic and yielding-malleable) behavior versus brittle in order to understand tectonics and fold belts on a truly global scale. We need to look toward fluid flow, as in plastic deformation in glaciers. Flowage is what we see when we stand back and look at mountains from a distance. Gravity is all pervasive in tectonics. It doesn't need to involve landslides; gravity gliding is sufficient." (Price, R., Geocanada 2000 Conference, Calgary)

> *"Which removeth the mountains, and they know not: which overturneth them in his anger."* (Job 9:5)

> *"Oh that thou wouldest rend the heavens, that thou wouldest come down, that the mountains might flow down at thy presence,...When thou didst terrible things which we looked not for, thou camest down, the mountains flowed down at thy presence."* (Isaiah 64:1, 3)

Both of these secular geologist's conclusions are in agreement with Scripture when they say that "ductile behavior" or plastic flowage explains the complex folding in our mountains and along the continental margins. However, they hold to the Darwinian and Lyellian idea of geologic time measured in millions and billions of years. The Rocky Mountains near Calgary is replete with tight folds in otherwise hard and brittle Paleozoic limestone. Thousands of feet of carbonates and shales were compressed into elongated fault and fold belts while still in an unlithified state and have since congealed into the hard and brittle rocks we see today. This type of mountain building could only happen if the formations were rapidly deposited and deformed very recently in time – within thousands, but not millions, of years!

The Alpine nappes are now deeply eroded, down to the roots in places, and covered by younger sediments and glaciers similar to the Canadian Rockies **(Figure 7)**.

Brilliant structural geologists spent their entire lifetimes unraveling these incredibly intricate structures, and yet they are still not fully understood. So complex are the overturned mountains that their original discoverer, Escher van der Linth, exclaimed in about 1844,

"No one would believe me if I published my sections; they would put me in an asylum." (Holmes, A., 1964, Principles of Physical Geology, p. 1162)

Albert Heim first published some of van der Linth's Alpine structural geological sections in 1875.

These mountain building processes are all described in the sublime, natural way characteristic of Scripture. It is God speaking to us in words we can comprehend in Psalm 46:2-3 (below). "Selah" means for the reader to stop and think or meditate on these words. Would to God that more people would do this when reading God's Word.

*"Therefore will not we fear, though the earth be removed, and though the mountains be carried into the midst of the sea; Though the waters thereof roar and be troubled, though the mountains shake with the swelling thereof. Selah."*

*"Mountains carried into the midst of the sea"* (Psalm 46:2c) would have involved swift gravity displacement of huge masses of semi-consolidated sediment into the foreland basins in front of the nappes. Tsunamis or tidal waves must have accompanied this collapse as it implies rapid movement due at least in part to faulting. Also, great debris flows would have cascaded into the seas as erosion cut into the rising nappes. The phrase, *"he overturneth the mountains by the roots"* is in context to, *"He cutteth out rivers among the rocks; and his eye seeth every precious thing."* (Job 28:9b-10) Rapid uplift presupposes that erosion and removal of the sediment and rock by rivers also lie within the timeline of Biblical chronology **(Figure 7c)**. Verse 10b suggests that valleys cut very deeply into the mountains, even into their roots. Geologist Arthur Holmes wrote concerning the Italian Pennine Alps,

"At least parts of the floor of the deep Ligurian Sea **rose** to great elevations at one time or another, like present day Corsica. Kuenen concludes, 'Here we have a striking and direct demonstration that a deep basin with 2500 meters of water was formerly a land area undergoing denudation from early Cretaceous to late Oligocene.' Large scale chaotic nappes like those of the northern Apennines have also been described from Timor and Turkey. In all these regions there have *been* rapid up-and-down movements accompanied by ophiolitic vulcanism, including serpentinites, indicative of wave-like alternations between highland ridges and deep sea troughs." (Holmes, A., 1964, Principles of Physical Geology, p. 1182)

Job lived to the south of present day mountainous Turkey. He spoke similar words to those in Holmes' extract above.

*"Behold, he withholdeth the waters, and they dry up: also he sendeth them out, and they overturn the earth. As the waters fail from the sea, and the flood decayeth and drieth up:"* (Job 12:15, 14:11)

A decaying flood is one that diminishes in a progressive and observable manner. The verse is not referring to a localized event but one compassing a large body of water – *"As the waters fail from the sea."* Job and his predecessors witnessed Mesozoic crustal deformation in modern in Chaldea and were privy to the more intense orogeny to the north.

The "days of Peleg" were a tumultuous period of flooding, upheaval and volcanic activity, both on land and in the newly-formed major ocean basins. They were the most geologically active part of earth history before recent times. On the chart of relative sea level rise this period forms Megacycle 3, second only to that of Megacycle 2 that began with Noah's Flood in 2348 B.C. **(Figure 1)**. The swelling of mountain roots involved profound uplift that brought hot magma nearer to the earth's surface, resulting in volcanism in some areas. Job and his peers viewed such upwelling of lava from within the fiery interior of the earth. They also knew that hell, the abode of departed lost souls, was down there. Jesus warned sinners many times of a burning hell in the New Testament.

> *"As for the earth, out of it cometh bread: and under it is turned up as it were fire."* (Job 28:5)
>
> *"It is as high as heaven; what canst thou do? deeper than hell; what canst thou know?"* (Job 11:8)
>
> "Everywhere in NE Africa between Egypt and Syria a major break separates the Jurassic and Cretaceous sequences: It is characterized by regional tilting, uplift and erosion, and by folding. Volcanics were extruded locally in northern Palestine." (Keeley, M., 1991, The Jurassic System in Northern Egypt, Journal of Petroleum Geology, pp. 49-64)
>
> "Other vast areas which were flooded with basalts in Jurassic or Tertiary times occur in...Arabia and Syria, in many parts of Africa...Altogether more than one million cubic miles of basalt have been transferred from the depths during the last 180 million years or so." (Holmes, A., 1964, Principles of Physical Geology, p. 300)

What was the general rate of uplift for these mountains given the constraint of Biblical chronology? Modern world encircling mountain ranges *were* formed during the "days of Peleg" when *"the earth was divided."* Some creation geologists attribute younger mountain building to Noah's Flood; the current writer places them in Peleg's days. In either case the striking mountain ranges of today, such as the Alps, Rockies and Himalayas, formed in recent times. They were raised up to their present heights in only a few hundred years' time. That translates to uplift of about seventy feet per year for the Alps and twice as much for the Himalayas. Far higher rates of uplift may have occurred because landmass fragments did not immediately collide as *"the earth divided."* Therefore, deformation was orders of magnitude greater than that postulated by modern uniformitarian geologists. Uplift and horizontal movement were at least seven to fifteen thousand times greater in magnitude than that measured today. What seems impossible to modern science is exactly the realm in which God works. Diastrophic entropy rapidly settled the mountains to their present tectonic stability. Hutton, Lyell were 'fooled' by their appearance of great age because they refused to believe God's Word. Darwin was "hooked" by Lyell's uniformitarianism.

# CHAPTER 5

## THE BOOK OF JOB AND CENOZOIC-MESOZOIC SEDIMENTATION

Strata comprising the Triassic, Jurassic, Cretaceous and Tertiary portions of the Geologic record were deposited during the last two hundred and forty-five million years according to uniformitarian geologists. Sediments accumulated in basins along the edges of continents and in seaways within them. The total thickness of rock in these areas commonly exceeds 10 kilometers. The author has worked on petroleum exploration projects where wells were drilled on both margins of the Atlantic Ocean, namely in the Scotian Basin (Canada) and the Senegal Basin (N. Africa). Therefore, **Figure 6b** is drawn from his personal experience in the oil industry.

> "Worldwide, a composite thickness of 70 kilometers has been measured." (Holmes, A., 1964, Principles of Physical Geology, p. 157)

An average rate of sedimentation of 0.23m/100 years is calculated by adhering to the theory of uniformitarianism.

Biblical chronology also limits the deposition of thick Cenozoic and Mesozoic sediments to the "days of Peleg," when *"the earth was divided"* **(Figure 2b)**. During a period of about 240 years the Bible describes the 'sea being divided', 'mountains overturned by the roots' and being 'removed and carried into the midst of the sea', 'waters failing from the sea' as well as 'floods decaying and mighty rivers drying up.' The past tense of the verb indicates the dividing of the earth was completed during Peleg's lifetime. All of these processes led to equally high rates of erosion and deposition during the same time period. Therefore, the whole concept of long ages for erosion and deposition of thick sedimentary formations is invalid. All of the requisite conditions existed for the deposition of vast thicknesses of sediment in widespread sedimentary basins all over the world. The same kind of processes operated during Noah's Flood and continued through the "days of Peleg" to the end of the Pleistocene glaciation following Peleg's days.

Peleg's earth was structurally and depositionally dynamic, containing near perfect conditions for rapid erosion and sedimentation. Basic environments and processes were comparable to those existing today. Yet, the rates of sediment accumulation were accelerated far beyond what we see in the modern world. Energy released from within the earth by the rupture of "the fountains of the great deep," and the earth expanding with mantle convection, was transformed into vastly superior, natural physical forces acting on the earth's crust, compared to what we see today. The release of energy started and carried on as accelerated seafloor spreading and continental drift through to the end of the "days of Peleg." Depositional systems were charged with this release of energy from within the earth. They functioned with incredibly rapid subsidence and basin filling, virtually indistinguishable from today's sedimentary environments and ecosystems. That is why it was so easy for geologists like Lyell to latch onto uniformitarianism. Clastic and carbonate sediments accumulated at rates ten-to-twenty thousand times higher than today. Nearly 4600 meters of sediments were deposited per century to accommodate the ten kilometers of Post-Paleozoic sedimentary strata along the continental margins bordering the Atlantic Ocean. The same pattern is observed worldwide for similar stratigraphic intervals in rapidly subsiding basins.

The Scriptures declare that God was in control of these depositional processes. "Mighty rivers" are part of major depositional systems that extend from the drainage basin to a lake, sea or ocean basin where vast quantities of sediments are deposited. They consisted of sandstones and shales in river channels, deltas, offshore bars and deep marine settings and calcium carbonate sediments in marine shelves, platforms, reefs and deep water environments.

> *"Thou didst cleave the fountain and the flood: thou driedst up mighty rivers."* (Psalm 74:15)

God broke up "the fountains of the great deep," and initiated the period of intense earth upheaval, erosion and deposition that continued into the "days of Peleg" when the earth "was divided." The geological 'column' records these two great events.

The author has studied Cenozoic and Mesozoic stratigraphy along the margins of eastern Canada and northwest Africa. He has examined both the well information and their correlation to the seismic sections. The eastern and western Atlantic continental shelves and slopes contain nearly identical sedimentary sections consisting of sandstone, shale, limestone and evaporites. **(Figure 6)** Rivers eroded the new landmasses, first filling rift valleys and later carrying sands and clays into the opening oceans. Many ancient river systems are now preserved only as sandstones and shales deep within the earth's crust. A mighty river once fed the Lower Cretaceous-Upper Jurassic delta near Sable Island, Nova Scotia, that forms the principal reservoir for East Coast geo-pressured gas fields and some oil deposits. There are many examples of tensional faulting and gravity flowage in these sedimentary wedges. Rivers along the continental margins poured great thicknesses of clastic sediment into deltas, beaches, offshore shelf clays and deep-water fans. In some areas great river systems remained relatively stable geographically until recent times, as in Senegal, while in others the channels dried up and disappeared. Jurassic limestones were also rapidly accumulating in the warm seas bordering the opening Atlantic's margins as "the earth was divided." Corals and other lime-secreting organisms proliferated in the shallow tropical waters along the Jurassic and Lower Cretaceous coastlines nourished by the rich supply of minerals from the upwelling mid-ocean ridges. Great carbonate platforms, resembling the modern Bahama Banks, rimmed both sides of the opening Atlantic Ocean and attained a thickness of more than thirty-five hundred meters. They are found in the subsurface offshore of the U.S. and Maritime Canadian coasts, and in basins along the coast of northwest Africa. Structures in both these sandstone-shale and limestone formations are easily mapped by geophysical methods. Discrete environments of deposition occur within the rock formations that can be compared with analogues in modern depositional environments around the world. Despite the rate of deposition the sedimentary rock types look alike.

Thick depositional systems that can be mapped geologically and on seismic lie buried along the continental margins and in interior basins on all continents. They formed in hundreds and not millions of years of time between Noah's Flood and the end of "the days of Peleg," a period of about 350 to 400 years in the recent past. That is THE reason why we find carbon 14 throughout these sediments and in the fossil fuels found in them. That is THE reason why we find dinosaur bones with soft tissues throughout the world in such sedimentary basins and depositional systems. God controlled the "mighty rivers" and everything associated with them, including the uplifted mountains and subsiding basins. Truly, this is an amazing fact, based upon secular science and the declaration of Scripture – both being in agreement that the worldwide composite geological 'column' was deposited in a very short period of time as shown in **Figure 1**. Some of Paleozoic basins were ruptured during Peleg's time. One example known to the writer has one part in Brazil and the other in southwestern Africa. When the two continents are joined to their pre-drift position the full basin configuration becomes apparent together with its depositional framework.

Similar Mesozoic sediments accumulated along the Tethys Sea to the north and east of the Land of Uz where Job lived **(Figure 4)**. They later became deeply buried oil and gas reservoirs that now host some of the world's largest hydrocarbon reserves. The Ghawar Oil Field in Saudi Arabia is in Jurassic limestones while the Burgan Field of Kuwait is mainly in Cretaceous shoreline sandstones that originated from a "mighty river," the ancestral Euphrates. The sea has since decayed and dried up as the Bible describes.

The ancestral Mediterranean Sea had great accumulations of limestone that formed massive sponge reefs during the Jurassic and Cretaceous periods. Until recently, they were considered relicts of the past. In 1999, a remarkable discovery was made in two hundred and fifty meters of water off the coast of British Columbia. 'Jurassic' reefs are still alive and thriving in the waters of the Pacific Ocean!

> "Unique colonies of giant sea sponges living off the B.C. coast are like time machines for researchers, who say the living fossils offer a glimpse into history that is unavailable anywhere else on the planet. It is as if they had discovered an island where dinosaurs somehow survived, undetected, to the present day, said Kim Conway of the Geological Survey of Canada...(The sponges) live in massive groups as they did 65 million years ago...when Tyrannosaurus Rex walked the Earth. "It's a living fossil and a way to explain much of southern Europe's geology from the Jurassic, which is when dinosaurs dominated the world," Conway said." (Simpson, S., March 31, 2001, Calgary Herald)

This discovery is not surprising because Biblical chronology puts the Jurassic reefs of Europe into recent earth history. Many more 'living fossils' must exist in today's seas. The *coelacanth*, a fossil fish from Paleozoic and Mesozoic strata, was recently found alive in the Pacific Ocean. It supposedly became extinct at the end of the Cretaceous Period 70 million years ago. 'Extinct' Paleozoic molluscs and crustaceans have also been found living in waters of the Atlantic.

> "Throw into this mix 'living fossils,' and the evolutionary picture gets quite fuzzy. These fossils are allegedly millions of years old, yet look extremely similar to descendants living today. The horseshoe crab has been around with basically the same configuration for 450 million years (?); dragon flies for 350 million years (?); jelly fish for 150 million years (?); the coelacanth fish for 400 million years (?) (Carter, R., 2014, Evolution's Achilles' Heels)

The conifer, *Metasequoia,* which was thought to have become extinct in the Miocene '20 million' years ago, is still living in a remote area of China. The *Tuatara* of New Zealand is living today, but is last seen as a fossil in the Early Cretaceous 'Valanginian,' supposedly 135 million years ago according to radiometric 'dating' methods (see **Table 5**, p. 126).

Cenozoic and Mesozoic sedimentary rocks record many variations in sea level. They were a response to changes in the rates of seafloor spreading and orogenic movements during 'the days of Peleg.' Job lived on stable continental crust comprising the Arabian Shield. Crustal rifting and seafloor spreading were occurring in the adjacent Tethys Sea. From this vantage he saw both rising and falling sea levels along its coastline and spoke,

> *"As the waters fail from the sea, and the flood decayeth and drieth up:"* (Job 14:11)

This verse means that there were periods of relatively higher and lower sea level during Job's day. Their record is preserved in the rocks as distinctive marine flooding deposits and shoaling sequences in the ancient Tethys sedimentary basin and rocks of a similar age around the world. Many, many such sedimentary cycles are recorded in the rock record following Noah's Flood. They record shifting depositional environments as the sea level rose and fell. The writer mapped these cycles in many basins as an important part of the oil and gas exploration methodology.

Looking at the worldwide so-called Geologic 'Column' in **Figure 1**, one thing becomes very apparent. There are two major megacycles of rising sea level each capped by a maximum low level stand of sea level. These two megacycles, 2 and 3, comprise the two great episodes of erosion and deposition in world history, namely Noah's Flood and "the days of Peleg." All of our Late Precambrian, Paleozoic, Mesozoic and Cenozoic (Tertiary Period) fit into this great depositional framework, with the Pleistocene glaciation immediately following. Today, you would never know the "the present in NOT the key to the past."

Mountain building and sedimentation are interrelated. Uplift creates erosion that in turn produces clastic material to be transported in rivers and carried to the coastline where paralic environments such as deltas and offshore bars are found.

High rates of erosion in the uplifted areas and rapid subsidence in the sedimentary basin or basins adjoining them can lead to very thick sedimentary deposits. It is God who controlled these processes and was ultimately responsible for the observed geological phenomena that we see preserved in the rock record and the mountain belts of the world. It is unfortunate that few geologists will acknowledge God's hand in forming the rock record. When the disciples witnessed Jesus' power on the Sea of Galilee they could only say with awe and fear:

> *"And there arose a great storm of wind, and the waves beat into the ship, so that it was now full. And they awake him, and say unto him, Master, carest thou not that perish? And he arose, and rebuked the wind, and said unto the sea, Peace, be still. And the wind ceased, and there was a great calm. And they feared exceedingly, and said one to another,* ***What manner of man is this, that even the wind and the sea obey him?****"* (Mark 4:37-39, 41)

> *"He putteth forth his hand upon the rock; he overturneth the mountains by the roots."* (Job 28:9)

God's power is revealed in the Biblical chronology, and not geologic time. Darwin robbed God of the glory due to His name. He denied the Holy One of Israel who designed these wonderful things and brought them to pass. Within this divinely documented time frame occurred catastrophic earth movements and their accompanying geologic processes. The Holy Bible describes the physical earth perfectly adequately. The Son of God, Jesus Christ, was the active mover and final authority, not Hutton, Lyell or Darwin. The Creator was the Lord Jesus Christ, the Son of God. He is still in control (Colossians 1:16-17). Charles Darwin never mentioned Him once by name in his original 545 page edition of *"On the Origin of Species."* How terrifying to meet Jesus Christ having denied Him in over five hundred pages of human-reasoned speculations about the origin of biological life and the effect of earth processes on biological life!

> *"And to make all men see what is the fellowship of the mystery, which from the beginning of the world hath been hid in God, who created all things by Jesus Christ:* (Ephesians 3:9)

So, all that we see in the earth today is the handiwork of God, done in His way, and in His time. Included in these wonders are the supposedly extinct dinosaurs living within the context of Biblical chronology when tropical environments were widespread across many parts of the world. Dinosaurs are a children's favorite and a fascination for all. Yet, they lived within human history during Job's lifetime and likely for many centuries afterward.

# CHAPTER 6

## THE BOOK OF JOB AND THE DINOSAURS

Few subjects arouse more general interest among all ages today than dinosaurs. Museums, comic books and movies depict these creatures enthralling adults and children alike. The fascination surrounding them stems from their size, ferocity and sudden disappearance, or supposed extinction sixty-five million years ago at the end of the Cretaceous Period. Dinosaurs are one of the strongest tools used by academia and the media to indoctrinate people in Darwinian evolution and an anti-Biblical bias, when the Word of God places them within the Biblical chronology after Noah's Flood. Children are especially vulnerable to this kind of deception.

Two twenty-first century dino-spectaculars, *Jurassic Park* and *The Lost World*, made dinosaurs 'come back to life' through computerized animation. Watching these movies made the viewers feel that they were living back in the Jurassic Period. The producers were careful to emphasize 'one hundred and fifty million years ago.' But did the dinosaurs really live that far back in the past? Biblical chronology gives an emphatic, "NO!" Job witnessed living dinosaurs about four thousand one hundred years ago. Let us look at the evidence.

The setting for the Book of Job is in the land of Uz where its principal subject is undergoing a severe testing, allowed by God, at the hand of the devil, Satan. Job was a landowner and herdsman, so there were great expanses of plain and some cities in the area in which he lived. His physical condition had become so pitiful that no one wanted him near. Even the poorest of people who inhabited the desolate wilderness reviled and spat upon him. So he was exiled to a lonely place where he suffered with minimal human contact. Job himself describes the setting as solitary.

*"I am a brother to dragons, and a companion to owls."* (Job 30:29)

He was in a place near to **dragons**. What are these *"dragons"* or *"tanniyn"* as they are called in the Hebrew? The closest dictionary definition is 'terrible monster' and refers to both land and sea types. *"Leviathan"* of Job Chapter 41 was a terrible sea monster without equal on the earth. Were these creatures imagined or real? The Scripture says that they were real and known to Job and others of his day.

The word **dragon** is mentioned twenty times in the Bible in relation to a specific type of animal and always in reference to the wilderness, meaning a lonely place apart from human habitation. Listed below are several references to the "dragons" that are described as living in Biblical times. They once lived in the land of Edom to the east of Sinai, and many other places in the Middle East and Mesopotamia. They are mentioned only once in the Book of Job indicating they were far longer-lived than Job's life span alone.

***"And I hated Esau, and laid his mountains and his heritage waste for the dragons of the wilderness."*** (Malachi 1:3)

***"Though thou hast sore broken us in the place of dragons, and covered us with the shadow of death."*** (Psalm 44:19)

*"Nebuchadnezzar the king of Babylon hath devoured me, he hath crushed me, he hath made me an empty vessel, he hath swallowed me up like a dragon, he hath filled his belly with my delicates, he hath cast me out."* (Jeremiah 51:34)

*"And the wild asses did stand in the high places, they snuffed up the wind like dragons; their eyes did fail, because there was no grass."* (Jeremiah 14:6)

*"Therefore I will wail and howl, I will go stripped and naked: I will make a wailing like the dragons, and mourning as the owls."* (Micah 1:8)

These verses read like an excerpt from *Jurassic Park* and not like a scene depicting modern small reptiles or foxes. Picture men being *"sore broken—in the place of dragons,"* in a solitary wilderness. Imagine them being *"swallowed—up"* by huge land monsters similar to those unfortunates who were ingested whole by a *T. Rex* in *Jurassic Park* and its sequel. On the back cover of this book is a thin section from a *Nanotyrannus* showing bone building cells (osteocytes) in soft bone tissue. Imagine watching the great reptiles 'smelling the winds' for enemies or for victims and their 'piercing wails' as they communicated, much as baby crocodiles do today. If these dragons are indeed the ancient dinosaurs, is one described in the Bible? Yes, a dinosaur is described in God's Word, and one that causes the greatest fascination for all because of its size.

Job 40:15-24 is a detailed description of an animal unlike anything living on the earth today. It is not conjured from fancy or the imagination because the picture is too specific and accurate. The LORD is making His servant, Job, clearly understand His power and glory in the realm of creation by describing *"**behemoth.**"* God speaks to Job *"in the place of dragons,"* where he can see *"behemoth."* In Chapter 40, verse 15a-b, we read, *"Behold now behemoth, which I made with thee."* Imagine Job looking at behemoth and then following the detailed description given by God as the Creator fully describes that great creature and its habitat. **Table 3** presents ten verses in their grammatical segments and sequential order, interpreting them relative to an artist's view in **Figure 9**.

| JOB 40 | EVIDENCE FROM SCRIPTURE | INTERPRETATION OF THE EVIDENCE |
|---|---|---|
| 15a | *Behold now behemoth,* | Job, look at the enormous animal (**behemoth**). |
| 15b | *which I made with thee;* | I made this animal at the same time as you, Job. |

| | | |
|---|---|---|
| 15c | *he eateth grass as an ox.* | He eats grass in a form of grazing. |
| 16a | *Lo now, his strength is in his loins,* | His strength is in the hips and lower abdomen. |
| 16b | *and his force is in the navel of his belly.* | His energy and power is in the center of his abdomen. |
| 17a | *He moveth his tail like a cedar:* | His tail is large and can be swayed like a huge tree. |
| 17b | *the sinews of his stones are wrapped together.* | He has thick layers of muscle encasing his bones. |
| 18a | *His bones are as strong pieces of brass;* | His bones are strong like a hard metal. |
| 18b | *his bones are like bars of iron.* | His bones and skeletal structure are hard and strong. |
| 19a | *He is the chief of the ways of God:* | He is the largest of God's creatures. |
| 19b | *he that made him can make his sword to approach unto him.* | God can kill **behemoth** through any destructive agent (i.e. **sword**), |
| | | likely including man. |
| 20a | *Surely the mountains bring him forth food,* | He lives near the mountains, along a river or coastal plain. |
| 20b | *where all the beasts of the field play.* | Many other animals live in the same open area. |
| 21 | *He lieth under the shady trees,* | He rests and is sheltered in wet, forested swamps. |
| | *in the covert of the reed, and fens.* | He is protected in long grasses of a wet, flat marshland. |
| 22a | *The shady trees cover him with their shadow;* | His habitat also contains large, closely-spaced trees. |
| 22b | *the willows of the brook compass him about.* | He lives near the shore, and sometimes moves on land. |

| | | |
|---|---|---|
| 23a | *Behold, he drinketh up a river,* | He has an enormous body cavity. |
| 23b | *and hasteth not:* | He moves slowly. |
| 23c | he trusteth that he can draw up Jordan into his mouth. | He is large enough to drink up a whole river. |
| 24a | He taketh it with his eyes: | He has clear eyesight (and a long, moveable neck?) |
| 24b | his nose pierceth through snares. | His head is small in proportion to his body? He has a long neck. He is snared by hunters (man) |

**Table 3**

The Interpretation and Identity of **"behemoth"** from Job 40:15-24

**Table 3** is constructed to provide a systematic verse-by-verse interpretation of the attributes of "***behemoth.***" It is necessary to examine the Scriptures very carefully because God does not waste words. His description to Job is comprehensive and involves skeletal structure, anatomy, living habits, environment and cause of death for this giant beast. **Table 4** is a correlation of the Scriptural and the secular information. Behemoth is definitely not a modern species of any living animal we know of today, but one that has an analogue in the past. The sauropod dinosaurs are the only creature that bears any resemblance to the animal described in Job 40:15-24. The recent discovery of *Paralititan stromeri* in the Western Sahara of Egypt provides skeletal remains consistent with the beast described in the Book of Job. It is a Cretaceous sauropod that lived on a coastal plain adjacent to the ancient Tethys Sea, an ancestor of the modern Mediterranean Sea. This ancient coastline passed through the area where Job lived, and is shown on the regional paleogeographic map of Syria and Iraq **(Figure 4)**.

**Figure 9** is a conceptual drawing based upon the information in **Table 3**. Its prospect is toward the south looking alongshore toward Egypt. The picture was drawn honoring the text like a police artist sketching a suspect's face. The verbal witness in this case is the Word of God.

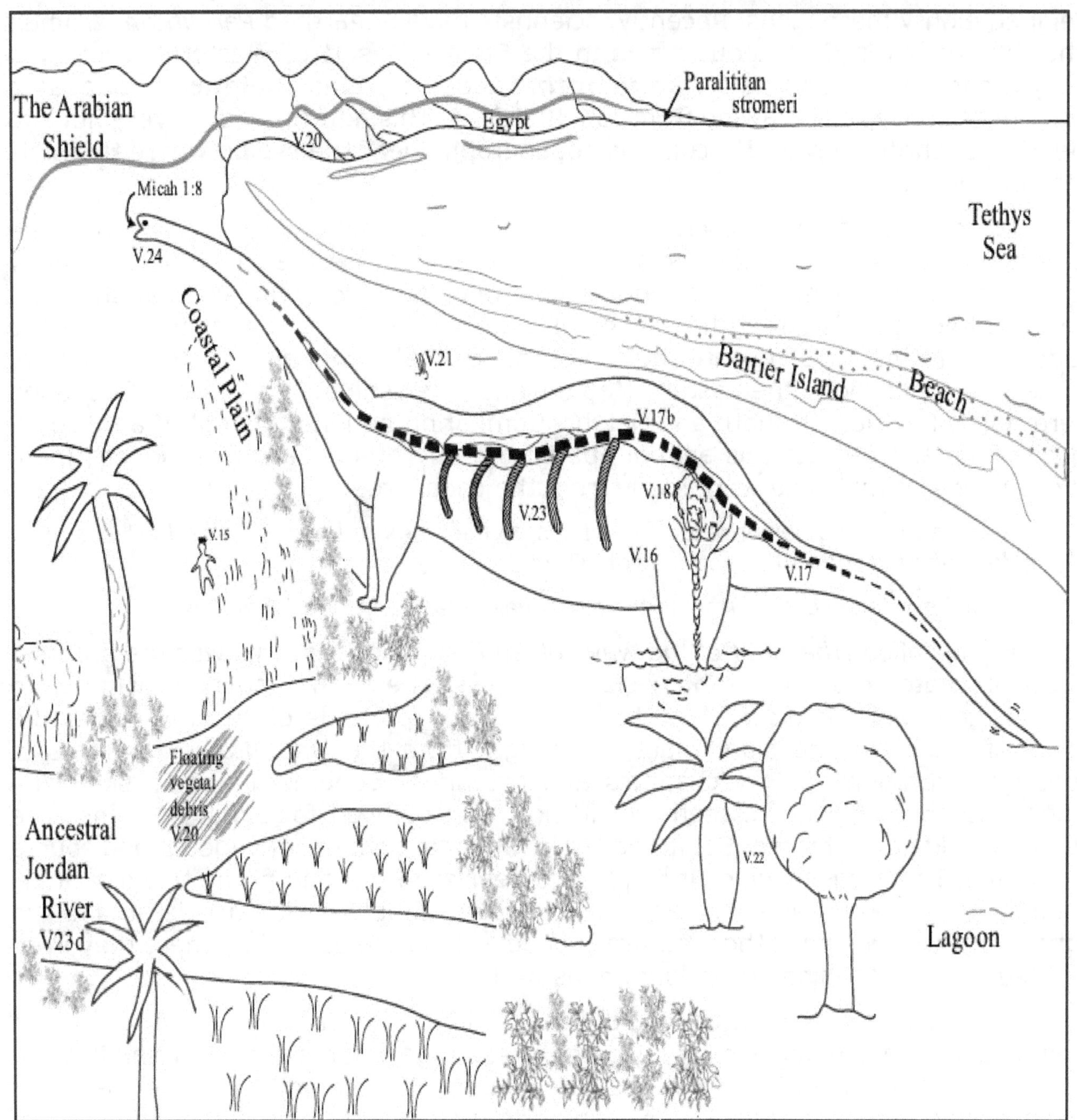


**Figure 9**

An Artist's depiction of **"behemoth"** taken from Job Chapter 40:15-24

Long-necked browsing dinosaur skeletons are the most spectacular fossil exhibits in modern museums. These sauropods were the largest four-legged animals to have lived, reaching gigantic proportions. In 1986, *Seismosaurus* was discovered in New Mexico. It was one hundred and thirty feet (40 meters) long, with individual vertebrae 5 feet in length and a shoulder blade eight feet high! Another beast from East Africa, *Brachiosaurus*, was seventy-five feet long, forty-one feet high, and weighed eighty metric tons. Recently, scientists have unearthed *Paralititan stromeri* (the tidal giant) in Cretaceous strata in the Sahara Desert of Western Egypt. It is likely the fossilized remains of ***"behemoth,"*** and is depicted in **Figure 9** (above) in the artist's conceptual drawing from Job 40:15-24. This new fossil discovery fits into the Biblical chronology and secular paleogeography near the region where the Bible patriarch Job lived.

We can make good descriptive sense of the animal and its habitat from the passage in Job 40. Behemoth was an enormous creature that lived in a swampy coastal plain environment bordering a mountainous region. His skeletal structure was massive and his strength was concentrated in his loins or rear portion of the body to carry his huge weight. The tail of this animal *"moved like a cedar,"* one of the largest trees along the eastern Mediterranean coastline. The cedars of Lebanon were noted for their strength and height. Comparing behemoth's tail to a 40 to 50 foot-tall cedar tree sets this animal apart from any other known to modern man. Ship's masts at that time were made from the cedar tree.

> *"I come up to the height of the mountains, to the sides of Lebanon; and I will cut down the tall cedars thereof,"* (Isaiah 37:24)
>
> *"they have taken cedars from Lebanon to make masts for thee."* (Ezekiel 27:5)

Being called *"the chief of the ways of God"* signifies that this was the greatest of God's created creatures in body size and mass. The animal moved slowly due to its enormous bulk, and preferred to lie in *"shady"* portions of swamps under the cover of trees. He ate plant material brought from the *"mountains"* as mats of floating vegetation in river channels and estuaries. Behemoth's small skull and limited number of peg-like teeth would not have sufficed for simple grazing; the animal would have starved. So, it needed an abundant source of vegetal food source to survive. The areas in which it lived were near sea level and prone to exceptional flooding when high rates of seafloor spreading coupled with accelerated basin subsidence overwhelmed the creatures in and around the estuaries where they lived and fed notwithstanding other dangers as well.

The fact that behemoth could *"draw* (drink) *up Jordan into his mouth,"* identifies a huge abdominal cavity used to ingest large volumes of water and floating vegetation as a part of its feeding pattern. Behemoth was not invincible. He could be destroyed by God's *"sword,"* which in Scripture is usually wielded by the hand of man or other predatory animals. Interestingly, a long neck with a small head, like a piercing 'arrow' in proportion to its body, is also indicated by the Scriptural wording; *"his nose pierceth through snares."* This body form made the animal vulnerable to man and to other flesh eating dinosaurs such as *T Rex*.

Man probably used snares to bring down "behemoth," because its small head and long neck could easily be dismembered or broken as it struggled to escape. Also, some formidable human beings lived in Job's day, ancestors of the ten-foot-tall giant, Goliath, whom David slew. They were descendants of Noah's son, Ham, and lived particularly in and around the land of Palestine and areas to the east, coinciding with the description of "behemoth's" habitat. These men reached heights of over ten feet and possessed incredible strength. They no doubt encountered the dragons mentioned in Scripture and were likely able to destroy them, when hunting in a group. God eventually exterminated these giants due to their sin.

> *"Yet destroyed I the Amorite before them, whose height was like the height of the cedars, and he was strong as the oaks; yet I destroyed his fruit from above and his roots from beneath."* (Amos 2:9)

Modern Bible interpreters suggest that ***"behemoth"*** was a 'water ox' or hippopotamus. A 'hippo' can't be drawn from this description, nor can an elephant or any other animal living today. The only beast that fits the Scriptural picture is a sauropod dinosaur, the group represented by types like *Apatosaurus (formerly Brontosaurus)* and *Brachiosaurus.* "No way," says the paleontologist! "This creature has been extinct for over sixty-five million years!" Has he really? Forget the narrative and face the facts! Remember that Job also gives accurate descriptions of great geological phenomena that coincide with the Jurassic and Cretaceous periods during which the dinosaurs lived. So why wouldn't there be a dinosaur in the text as well? **Table 4** brings the secular evidence (bold type) together with the Scriptural details (plain type), providing a direct scientific link between the sauropod species and the Biblical ***"behemoth."*** They are comparable to a very high degree in physiology, bone structure and environmental factors. Therefore, the evidence supports ***"behemoth"*** being a sauropod dinosaur living contemporaneous with man only a matter of four thousand years ago!

| I. PHYSICAL BODY | **Behold now behemoth, which I made with thee; He is the chief of the ways of God: (Job 40:15a,b; 19)** |
|---|---|
| a) Head and Neck | small head about 2 feet in length; extra-long neck — 30 feet plus in length |
| **Job 40:24b** | **his nose pierceth through snares.** |
| **Job 40:23; 24a** | **he trusteth that he can draw up Jordan into his mouth. He taketh it with his eyes.** |
| b) Body and Abdomen | long and deep body; enormous gut |
| **Job 40:23a, b** | **Behold, he drinketh up a river, and hasteth not:** |
| **Job 40:16a-c** | **Lo now, his strength is in his loins, and his force in the navel of his belly.** |
| c) Legs and Tail | large, pillar-like legs; long, thick tapering tail to 45 feet in length |
| **Job 40:17** | **He moveth his tail like a cedar:** |
| II. BONES AND MUSCLES | **the sinews of his stones are wrapped together. his bones are like bars of iron. (Job 40:17b; 18b)** |
| a) Whole Skeleton | masterpiece of engineering — lightweight framework made of immensely strong, yet flexible vertebrae |
| **Job 40:18a,b** | **His bones are as strong pieces of brass; his bones are like bars of iron.** |
| b) Skull | short, weak jaws with approximately 12 slim, peg-like teeth; skull often missing from rest of skeleton (see IV) |
| c) Backbone and Vertebrae | monumental construction required to carry enormous body and transfer weight to legs; massive vertebrae to 5 feet high |
| d) Hip Girdle | massive hip girdle firmly fused to backbone by 4 or 5 sacral vertebrae forming solid support for heavy body and tail |
| e) Pelvis | stoutly-constructed pelvis |
| **Job 40:16** | **Lo, now, his strength is in his loins, and his force is in the navel of his belly.** |
| f) Back muscles | interlacing series of ligaments and tendons passed between spines, helping to strengthen the back |
| **Job 40:17b** | **the sinews of his stones are wrapped together.** |
| III. ENVIRONMENT | Swampy coastal plain with rivers and lush vegetation |
| a) General Setting | lowland swampy areas and tropical river plains, estuaries and lagoons |
| **Job 40:20a; 21** | **Surely the mountains bring him forth food, He lieth under the shady trees, in the covert of the reed, and fens.** |
| b) Food Type | browsed on different kinds of plant material, probably consisting of floating mats of grasses eroded from the hinterland |
| **Job 40:15c; 20a; 23a, b** | **he eateth grass as an ox. Surely the mountains bring him forth food; Behold, he drinketh up river,** |
| c) Eating Limitation | dental and jaw apparatus insufficient for huge body; needed abundant, soft watery vegetation to eat with little effort |
| d) Preferred Habitat | in amphibious life browsing in lowland swamps and coastal lagoons near river channels |
| **Job 40:21; 22b** | **He lieth under the shady trees, in the covert of the reed and fens; the willows of the brook compass him about.** |
| IV. ENEMIES (incl. man) | **he that made him can make his sword approach unto him. his nose pierceth through snares. (Job 40:19b; 24b)** |

**Table 4**

Scriptural and secular scientific comparison between **"behemoth"** and sauropod dinosaurs

There is no animal like **"behemoth"** described in **Table 4**. It is completely unique! It is not an elephant, hippopotamus, crocodile or any other creature! The conceptual drawing in **Figure 9** shows a beast resembling a sauropod dinosaur. These animals supposedly became extinct tens of millions of years ago! Yet, the description in Job Chapter 40 **(Table 3)** is accurate in every detail, as **Table 4** shows. The two secular references used for the comparison are as follows: "*Vertebrate Paleontology,*" by Romer, A., 1967, U. of Chicago Press and "*Mac Millan Illustrated Encyclopedia of Dinosaurs and Prehistoric Animals,*" by Dixon D., et al, 1988, Mac Millan Publishing Company.

Harmonization between Scripture and geology confirms the Biblical chronology and refutes the secular theory of evolution. Nowhere is there a contradiction in the Bible, but only a verse by verse agreement with the specific scientific descriptions. The completed picture gives geology a Biblically-based time frame and ties the 'age of the dinosaurs' to "the days of Peleg,' a mere 4100 years ago! The following examples demonstrate this point:

> *"Thou didst divide the sea by thy strength: thou brakest the heads of the dragons in the waters. Thou brakest the heads of leviathan in pieces, and gavest him to be meat to the people inhabiting the wilderness. Thou didst cleave the fountain and the flood: thou driedst up mighty rivers."* (Psalm 74:13-15)

The ***"behemoth"*** text also correlates with the relevant portion of secular Mesozoic paleogeography for the Land of Uz in Job's time. The area between Chaldea and the Dead Sea, and adjoining the Jordan River contains Cretaceous sandstones that were deposited in a coastal plain environment similar to the one described in Job Chapter 40. That shoreline extended across Egypt. The paleogeographic map in **Figure 4** places the Lower Cretaceous well within Job's sphere of observation for sauropod dinosaurs in the region in which he lived. Men in the Post-Flood generations lived to see "mighty rivers" dried up. They lived long and witnessed highly accelerated rates of uplift, erosion and subsidence and sedimentation compared to today's geological processes.

Job's home lay along the Cretaceous coastal plain extending to the northeast of the Dead Sea toward the present day Euphrates River in eastern Syria and adjoining Iraq. Because God refers Job to the Jordan River in this passage, Job must have been familiar with Canaan and the Dead Sea area, but did not live there. Eliphaz the Temanite, one of Job's three friends, was from the region of Teman (Edom) along the southeastern shore of the Dead Sea. Bildad the Shuhite was evidently from Shuah located near the Euphrates River (Wigoder, G., 1986, Illustrated Dictionary and Concordance of the Bible). Job must have made contact with these men in his travels. He knew of the Jordan River (Job 40:23). The paleogeographic map shown in **Figure 4**, suggests that there was an ancestral Jordon River in Job's day, not too-far-different from later Biblical times and today. It may have flowed north into the Tethys Sea only later toward the south into the Dead Sea. **Figure 10** shows the kind of environment in which these great beasts lived.

A similar Cretaceous coastal plain with rivers and estuaries was present in the area surrounding Drumheller, Alberta. It was inhabited by a wide variety of dinosaurs, including sauropods. Flooding along this coastal plain that formed an interior seaway in western North America was a result of subsidence and rapid seafloor spreading that reached a peak of highest worldwide sea level in the Upper Cretaceous. The world famous concentration of dinosaur fossils correlates with this period of time in western North America and many parts of the world.

Some of the best 'whole' specimens of this extinct species occur in the Upper Cretaceous Dinosaur Park Formation near Drumheller, Alberta. The excellent quality of the remains in this area are attributed to

> "a wave of subsidence ...preceded the migrating (*deltaic*) lobe ...and an increased accommodation space in this part of the Alberta Basin ...in response to differential overthrust tectonics along the (*Rocky Mountain*) Cordillera. ...tidal effects were established far upstream in coast rivers (>150 km), and coastlines became dissected by estuaries (*with*) Short term (*high*) rates of vertical aggradation (*producing*) ...a high capacity sediment trap (*favouring*) ...the burial and preservation of ...whole dinosaur carcasses." (Eberth, D., 1994, Abstract in CSPG Reservoir, vol. 21, no. 2)

The evolutionary Tyrell Museum stands in the Drumheller badlands. It exhibits many kinds of fossils including dinosaurs, all described in context to Darwinian evolution. To the north of Drumheller is the Big Valley Creation Science Museum. The Darwinian museum received hundreds of millions of dollars of government funding; the God-honoring one received nothing. It is a sign of the times. Darwin reigns! (see Chapter 9)

**Figure 10**

Artist's paintings of sauropod dinosaurs in their interpreted natural setting

*"Behold, he drinketh up a river, and hasteth not: he trusteth that he can draw up Jordan into his mouth."* (Job 40:23)

Ahroni (1966) describes the depositional environments bordering the Land of Uz in Job's day. His description of the Cretaceous sedimentary deposits shows a habitat favorable for sauropod dinosaurs. The ancestral Jordan River flowed toward the north into the Tethys Sea. A broad, grassy coastal plain fringed the coastline where Job observed *"behemoth"* and extended westward into Egypt. This depositional environment is closely comparable to that described in Job 40 **(Table 3)**.

> "It was at the time the Lower and Upper Cretaceous (Albian-to-Lower Cenomanian) Kurnub Group sandstones were being laid down in continental-to-transitional marine environments in the area to the south and east of the Dead Sea. They were deposited by rivers flowing in a north-to-northwesterly direction from off the Transjordan and Sinai parts of the Arabo-Nubian Continent. A coastline lay in the vicinity of eastern Israel and the adjoining part of Jordan, with marine conditions being present to the northwest. Sandstone beds and non-marine shale and lignite are near the shoreline on the continental side. This is typical of a marshy environment along the margin of a continent having a gentle relief, such as existed in this area after the pre-Kurnub Group erosion period."

Confirmation of the presence of a huge Cretaceous sauropod dinosaur has just been made in the Sahara Desert along the same Tethys shoreline where Job lived. The dimensions of this monster are given in **Figure 11**. A recent article in the London Telegraph, *"Scientists unearth giant dino,"* stated the following:

> "A desert quest has uncovered one of the biggest creatures to have existed. The dinosaur was found in a corner of Egypt that paleontologists had ignored since the Second World War, after earlier German finds from the site were destroyed by Allied bombers. The skeleton is one of the largest uncovered in Africa from the Cretaceous period, between 146 million and 65 million years ago, and might be the second biggest dinosaur found. **Paralititan stromeri**, the "tidal giant" is thought to have grown to 30 meters, weighed up to 70 tonnes, and walked on feet more than five feet across in the ancient mangrove swamps that are now the Sahara Desert. The giant dinosaur is the first discovery reported from the site since 1935." (Reprinted in the Calgary Herald, June 1, 2001)

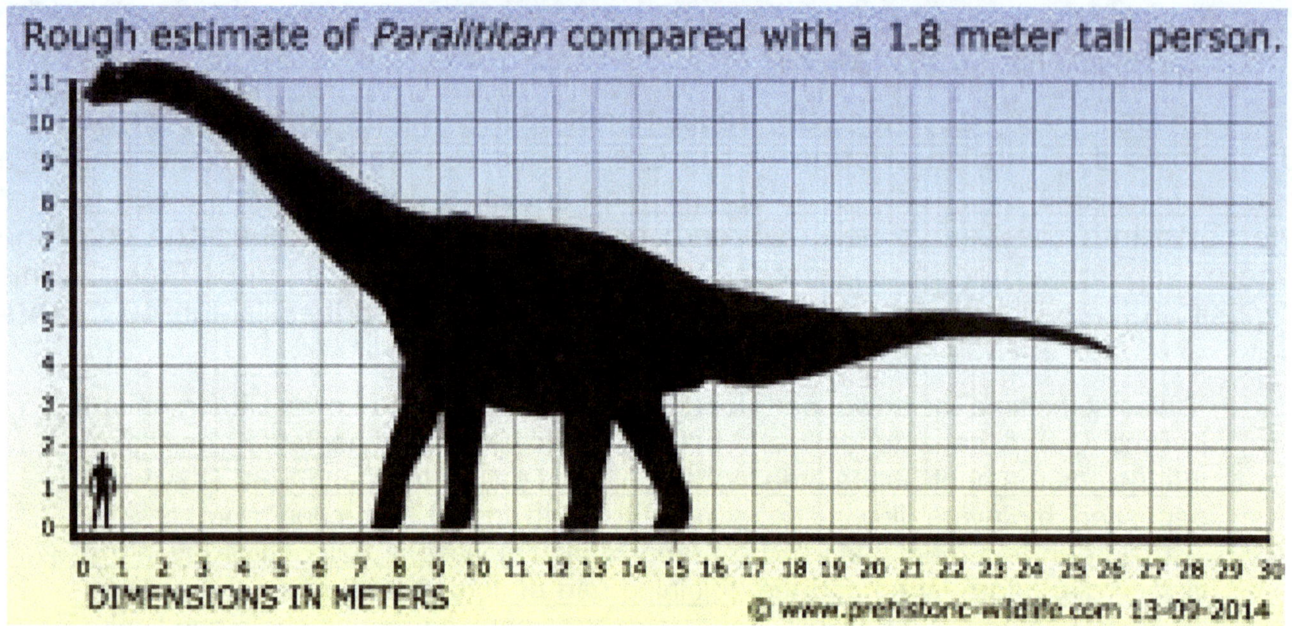


**Figure 11**

The dimensions of Paralititan compared to an average-sized human

The name "Paralititan" means literally the 'shoreline giant of enormous strength.' Its discoverer, Josh Smith, found the dinosaur site after entering the wrong coordinates on his GPS receiver and ending up far from the presumed location based upon old maps. "It was total serendipity," he said. Or was it? God led him there to give modern scientists a firsthand look at the remains of ***"behemoth"*** described with precise accuracy in the Book of Job, and along the same coastline to the west of where Job lived. By definition, the word ***"behemoth,"*** means "an enormous animal." (Winston Dictionary, 1946). Through these providential circumstances God is validating His Word and showing modern evolutionary scientists that their theory of evolution and calculation of the age of the earth are wrong. To drive this point home with unmistakable evidence dinosaur remains have been found recently that could NOT possibly be millions of years old!

> "For about a decade now there is mounting evidence of soft tissue still preserved in dinosaur bones. In 2005 the discovery of a dinosaur leg bone from *Tyrannosaurus Rex* showed still stretchy soft tissue, and different types of proteins. More material was discovered from a wide range of fossil animals from the so-called "Age of Dinosaurs." We've got *T Rex, Triceratops, a duck-billed dinosaur* – **even eggs containing unfossilized bones and organic molecules from sauropod dinosaurs from China**. Mounting evidence of soft tissues from multiple levels of rock from different continents are being identified by paleontologists." (Ross, M., 2014, Evolution's Achilles' Heels)

> "Filipodial extensions were delicate and showed no evidence of any permineralization or crystallization artifact and therefore were interpreted to be soft. This is the first report of sheets of soft tissues from Triceratops horn bearing layers

of osteocytes, and extends the range and type of dinosaur specimens known to contain non-fossilized material in bone matrix." (Armitage, M. and Anderson, K., 2013, Soft sheets of fibrillary bone from a fossil of the supraorbital horn of the (Upper Cretaceous, Campanian) dinosaur *Triceratops horridus*, Elsevier, Acta Histochemica 115, pp. 603-608)

Mark Armitage was fired from his position of Manager of California State University Northridge Biology Department's electron and confocal microscopy suite two weeks after publishing the above paper. He had engaged students about the possible age of the *Triceratops* horn, and one shared the conversation with a faculty member. Shortly after that, a faculty member entered his office and said, "We are not going to tolerate your religion in this department." Mr. Armitage was awarded a damage settlement in court for over $300,000 but his career at the university was destroyed. For what? Telling the truth.

"In 2013, a remarkable paper was published documenting the discovery of bone cells and DNA from dinosaur bones. DNA was proved from 3 independent chemical tests in the cell nucleus of a *T Rex*, including proteins called histones, where the DNA is coiled up in the cells-ruling out contamination. Even under ideal conditions, meaning temperatures well below freezing, DNA would not last anywhere near the 65 million years since dinosaurs were meant to have become extinct. Now in real life dinosaurs were to have lived in very warm climates, and warmth means DNA would decay even more quickly. **Therefore, the presence of DNA in dinosaur bones is <u>very strong evidence against millions of years of time scale</u>**." (Sarfati, J., 2014, Evolution's Achilles' Heels)

Speaking of these amazing finds, Paleontologist Dr. Mary Schweitzer stated in PBS/Nova Science Now in 2009, the following:

"When you think about it, the laws of chemistry and biology, and everything else that we know say that it should be gone; it should be degraded completely." (Ross, M., 2014, Evolution's Achilles' Heels)

That is, unless the dinosaur bones are thousands of years old, and not millions of years old! The *Triceratops* specimen mentioned above is from the Upper Cretaceous (Campanian) Hell Creek Fm. in South Dakota that is supposedly 80 million years old! A thin section of a N*anotyrannus lancensis* bone with soft tissues is shown on the back cover of this book. It was kindly provided by Ray Strom from Art Chadwick's studies in the Hell Creek Fm., Hanson Ranch, SD. This bone sample also displays soft tissue, bone-building cells (osteocytes) and blood vessels that have not been permineralized, similar to the *Triceratops* horn. Furthermore, the Drumheller dinosaur bones frequently contain some soft tissue, similar to the ones found in South Dakota, Montana and elsewhere (Ray Strom, personal communication). Mr. Strom has many samples of these bones in his lab. Some of the dinosaur fossil beds even emitted a cadaverous odor when excavated. After millions of years a rotting odor and soft tissues would be long, long gone.

Moreover, Cretaceous coals in the Drumheller area consistently contain the unstable radioactive isotope carbon-14, an element that is in unmeasurable amounts at ages of 80,000 to 100,000 years, even with the best of modern instruments. Therefore, the dinosaur fossils and the rocks within which they are interred CANNOT be millions of years old! The Lyellian and Darwinian mindset of millions and billions of years that has gripped 20$^{th}$ Century scientists is deeply flawed and patently WRONG! The radiometric 'dating' that gives these 'absolute' ages is WRONG! The only plausible explanation is that the Bible is giving the correct chronology for the age of the earth and the dinosaurs, and secular science is NOT. True science will take the scientific data at face value and look for the right answers through unbiased inquiry.

Correlation of ***"behemoth"*** with the Cretaceous *Paralititan stromeri* fits the Biblical timeline in **Figure 2** (p. 20). Job's estimated minimum age of 220 to 240 years in "the days of Peleg," together with his witness of *"behemoth"* indicates a time frame within the upper part of the Lower Cretaceous over four thousand one hundred years ago. That is why the dinosaur remains still contain soft tissues and DNA, and the Cretaceous coals show measurable $C^{14}$. Hence all of the data converge to put the geologic epochs within a Biblical, and not evolutionary, chronology. This observation is of profound importance. The Lord is giving confirmation of His Word for modern man. But will men listen? It is doubtful that they will because the issue is, faith in God's Word or an atheistic ideology based upon faith in man's word. The Darwinian scientists still remain onboard, though their ship is sinking.

*"God forbid: yea, let God be true, but every man a liar."* (Romans 3:4 pt.)

So Job's ***"behemoth"*** places beasts like *Paralititan, Apatosaurus* and *Brachiosaurus* in recorded human history and not in a pre-human evolving world. Other verses depicting dragons came from man's encounters with different types of dinosaurs such as *T Rex,* raptors and *Stegosaurus* (p. 52). Job Chapter 41 describes ***"leviathan,"*** a sea monster with the attributes of the extinct mosasaur or fish lizard from the same time period. The Tethys Sea lay north of the Land of Uz and contained deep seas where this creature would have thrived. Job was familiar with that beast also. God speaks to Job in specific detail about ***"leviathan"*** because Job knew what a frightening creature it was. Knowing that the great God who made this sea monster was speaking in Person to him out of the whirlwind humbled Job that much more. We in the twenty-first century, scientists or not, need humbling. It may be just around the corner.

Dinosaurs and *leviathan* lived about forty-three centuries in the past. How long they continued we do not know, except cultures around the world have carvings and drawings of them made long after the Flood was over. Scientists must reevaluate their entire philosophy for defining earth history. The foundation of our Western civilization depends upon a proper interpretation of our origins, which includes Creation, the fall of man, Noah's Flood and the days of Peleg. If God's Word is not taken into account in man's origin then men are just beasts and can live and act without any regard to a divine imperative and moral laws. In fact, that is why creationists are ostracized by Darwinian evolutionists.

Dinosaurs lived before the Flood but their fossil record has been completely destroyed, as was all other life by the sheer force of that cataclysm. They exited the ark with all the other flood survivors and moved out to cover the land area of Pangaea before the break-up of that great continent. That is why dinosaurs as well as other species of mammals and reptiles are found in both the eastern and western hemispheres despite the wide oceans separating them. God's timing was perfect in repopulating the earth and then separating the continents during Peleg's days to slow down the devastating consequences of mankind's corporate sinful condition. We are once again reaching the climax of man's rebellion against God and the gathering storm of another cataclysm is approaching.

One of the obstacles to interpreting modern history from a Biblical perspective has been glaciation. How could the Pleistocene ice advance and retreat so quickly, so many times, if the earth is only thousands of years old? Again, the Book of Job and other Scriptures will give us insight.

# CHAPTER 7

## THE BOOK OF JOB AND THE PLEISTOCENE ICE AGE

Modern evolutionary science teaches that the Pleistocene Epoch began about two million years ago when glaciers covered much of the Northern Hemisphere **(Figure 12a)** in Europe and North America, as well as large areas of the Southern Hemisphere. About 18 million square miles of the earth's surface was mantled with ice hundreds or thousands of feet thick. About two-thirds of it was in North America and Eurasia occupying mountain valleys and broad areas of the continents. Ice sheets attained thicknesses up to 14,000 feet in some areas and still cover vast areas such as Greenland and Antarctica. Remnants of mountain glaciers are present in the Rocky Mountains between Lake Louise and Jasper, Alberta. Glacial sediments, ice markings and landforms cover all of Canada and parts of the northern United States as relicts of this great climatic Arctic period. Pleistocene geologists believe that the ice took thousands of years to advance and retreat, and that several such cycles took place during the Pleistocene epoch beginning about 2 million years ago. They say we are in an inter-glacial period and glaciers are retreating in the Northern Hemisphere with a few exceptions. Scientists use the slow flow rates for modern glaciers and their past wide distribution as secular evidence for a long 'Ice Age,' again relying on uniformitarian principles and a Darwinian narrative.

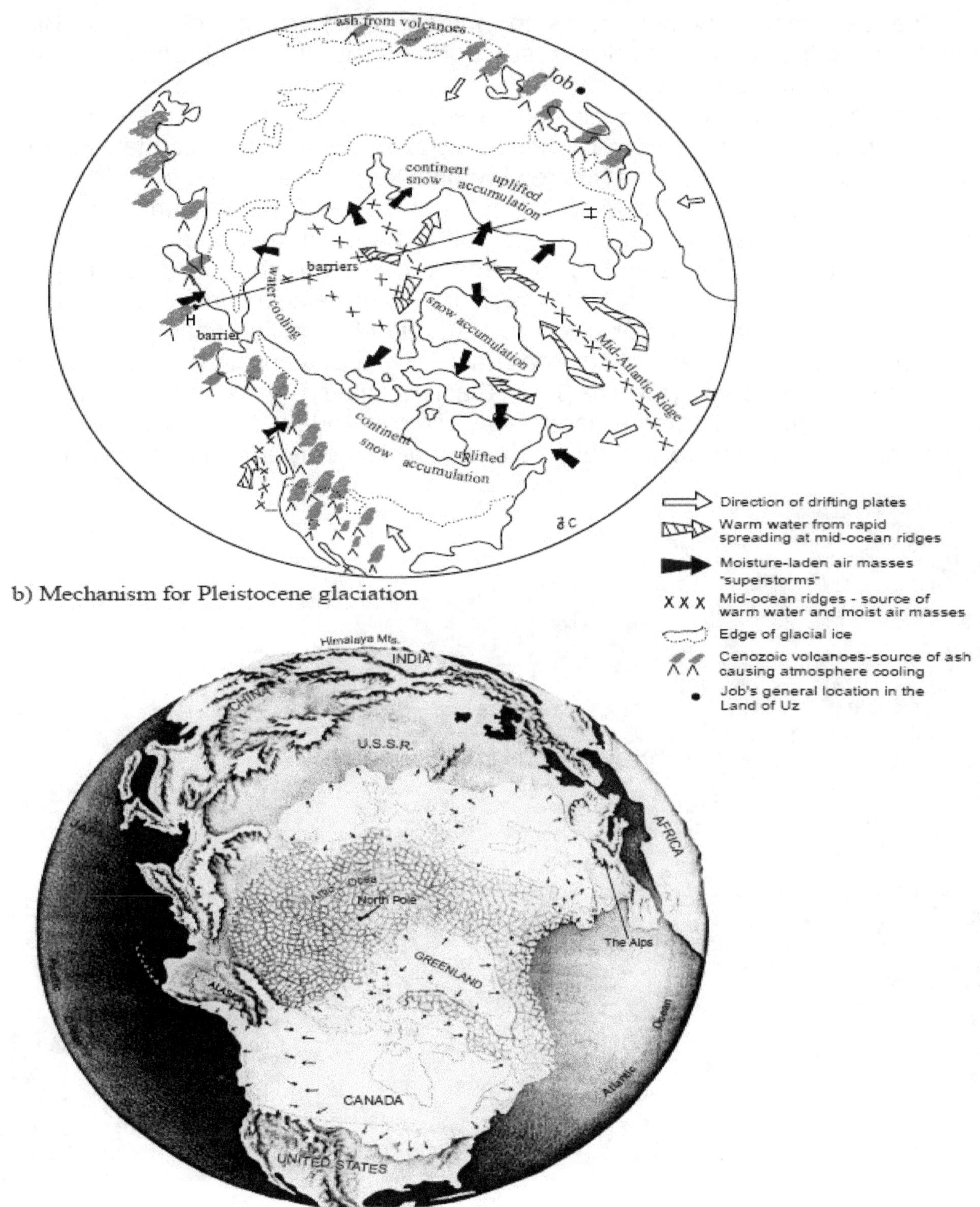


b) Mechanism for Pleistocene glaciation

a) Distribution of Pleistocene glaciers in the Northern Hemisphere (from Longwell and Flint, 1965)

**Figure 12**

Distribution and interpreted cause of Pleistocene glaciation in context to the Biblical chronology
Cross-section H – I on **Figure 12b** is shown on **Figure 14 (p. 75)**

The extremely low flow rates in modern glaciers do not negate Biblical chronology. Scripture imposes time restrictions on the Pleistocene just as it did on seafloor spreading, sedimentation and mountain building. If many 'orders of magnitude' higher rates of processes operated in the shaping of the earth then they must also have occurred during the Pleistocene Ice Age. The fact that sediments could accumulate and deform at incredibly high rates means snow could similarly form vast glaciers, since it is a wind-born crystal that accumulates and compacts to make a rock-like substance, ice. This ice had a powerful impact on the landscape. It filled mountainous regions and sculptured the rocks into sharp and ragged peaks, giving a semblance of long periods of erosion. Yet, the Pleistocene glaciers did their chiseling of the rock in a matter of centuries and not 2 million years as claimed by secular scientists. A dramatic picture shows such glaciers on the side of Mt. Victoria in the Canadian Rockies **(Figure 13)**. Glaciers filled the mountain valleys and carved the steep, mountainous landscape we see today. They had tremendous capacity for 'cutting' into rocks that had been uplifted only a short time before.

**Figure 13**

Mt. Victoria, 3464 m., showing glaciers in the Bow Range at Lake Louise, Alberta, from the top of Pope's Peak, 3163 m. (photo by F.C., 1980)

Glaciation began at or near the end of the days of Peleg when rapid seafloor spreading had begun to wind down. It lasted for several centuries, with the ice retreating off most of the Northern Hemisphere by about 1500 B.C. Therefore, man also witnessed and knew of the last 'Ice Age.' The Biblical evidence will be presented in subsequent paragraphs.

First we need to understand some basic facts about glaciers. They are solid masses of ice that develop in regions where snow accumulation exceeds melting. When 200 to 300 feet of ice has built up burial and compaction cause it to recrystallize, and individual crystals begin to slide one against the other like rolling marbles. The thick mass of ice, a glacier, deforms internally and flows as a plastic solid much like pancake batter on a griddle. Flowage occurs radially outward and downslope under the influence of gravity and the lateral forces exerted by the thick mass of ice in the accumulation center. Modern glaciers advance from a few feet per day to up to sixty feet per day.

Is there Biblical evidence for glaciers? To answer this question we must find Bible references concerning snow and ice and see if they can be interpreted in context to glaciation. Let us begin in the Book of Genesis. There was no precipitation in the form of rain before Noah's Flood according to Genesis 2:5c and 6,

> *"for the LORD God had not caused it to rain upon the earth…But there went up a mist from the earth, and watered the whole face of the ground."* (Genesis 2:5c – 6)

A vapor canopy was present above the atmosphere, creating a greenhouse climate devoid of rain over the whole earth. Subterranean waters "from the fountains of the great deep" supplied surface springs and mist to nurture the ground and its vegetation. Therefore, Pre-Flood Early Precambrian sedimentary rocks do not contain raindrop prints or glacial features caused by atmospheric weather cycles. The 20,000 foot-thick Late Precambrian sedimentary Torridonian series in Northern Scotland is interpreted as alluvial fan deposited along a mountain front. Red shale beds in the Torridonian contain distinct rain drop prints and fossilized mud cracks indicating rainfall and sub-aerial deposition in Late Precambrian mudflats. (Allen, P., in Crawford, F. ed., 1972, Arenaceous Deposits, Sedimentation and Diagenesis). The Torridonian rocks overlie the Early Precambrian granitic and metamorphic shield capped by a weathered, reddish clay representing a paleo-laterite soil horizon originally formed in a tropical to sub-tropical climate. This sedimentary contact is interpreted to be the Pre-Flood land surface overlain by the onset of Flood deposition, the alluvial fans being deposited as a part of the break-up and faulting along the "fountains of the great deep." The 12,000 foot-thick Hataki Shale of the Late Precambrian Grand Canyon series, Colorado, also contains raindrop prints and mudcracks similar to the Torridonian.

> *"In the six hundredth year of Noah's life, in the second month, the seventeenth day of the month, the same day were all the fountains of the great deep broken up, and the windows of heaven were opened. And the rain was upon the earth forty days and forty nights."* (Genesis 7:11-12)

Noah's Flood was the first time it rained on the earth. The rain and snow fell with overwhelming intensity during the initial forty days of the Flood 'year' when *"all the fountains of the great deep were broken up, and the windows of heaven were opened."* (Genesis 7:11d-e) During this short period thick Middle and Late Precambrian sediments were deposited over the ruptured earth. Evidence of Late Precambrian and Paleozoic glaciations reflect the release of enormous amounts of snow in some areas during the Flood Year, and between it and the onset of the days of Peleg. The Huronian Gowganda ('Tillite') Fm. contains at least 4 glacial advances (Douglas, R., 1969, Geology and Economic Minerals of Canada, p. 115). Exhumed remnants of Early Paleozoic glacial landforms and sedimentary deposits occur in the Chad-Niger part of Sahara Desert (Ibid). They are Upper Ordovician in 'age' and display 1000 foot-deep, U-shaped glaciated valleys, drumlins, eskers, hanging valleys, glacial sediments such as tillites, and marine beds containing 'dropstones' where the ice calved into the sea. More glaciations are recognized in the geologic record in different parts of the world coincident with catastrophic earth processes during and after Noah's Flood. God used both rain and snow in judging and cleansing the antediluvian world. The destruction was complete. Nothing remained of that early, God-denying advanced civilization, except Noah and his family, and the creatures with him in the Ark. The most recent Pleistocene glaciation was not designed to destroy the world but was a result of rapid seafloor spreading, mountain building and volcanism that concluded "the days of Peleg."

God promised never again to destroy the world by a great flood (Genesis 9:11). For this reason, there will be no more great floods of water or ice ages in the future. They began with Noah's Flood and ended with the Pleistocene ice age. God's next judgment on mankind will be by fire. Why? Because man has again rejected God and His Word, as he did in Noah's day.

Considering the scale and destruction wrought by Noah's Flood it is a miracle that the tiny ark survived the raging elements of wind and wave. Only the protective hand of Almighty God safely steered Noah's tiny bark through that 'Storm' of all storms amid calamitous flooding, surging glaciers and colliding blocks of continental crust. So the waters that had prevailed to destroy man for his sin began to abate in order that life would be preserved and renewed on the earth; man being given another opportunity to obey and serve God through Noah and his descendants.

> *"And God remembered Noah, and every living thing, and all the cattle that was with him in the ark: and God made a wind to pass over the earth, and the waters asswaged;"* (Genesis 8:1)

Scripture first mentions a regular climatic cycle of summer and winter just after Noah leaves the Ark.

> *"While the earth remaineth, seedtime and harvest, and cold and heat, and summer and winter, and day and night shall not cease."* (Genesis 8:22)

Following the Flood, mountainous terrain and vast ocean basins formed, initiating the regular hydrologic cycle mentioned in Ecclesiastes 1:6-7. Sediment laden rivers became the norm replacing the quiescent conditions of the Pre-Flood tropical world. Thick sedimentary deposits accumulated within basins formed on the Post-Flood supercontinent, Pangaea, and in rapidly subsiding basins along its margins. These rocks belong mainly to the Paleozoic Period. With climatic variation came rain and snow, including their natural by products, rivers and floods, and continental and mountain glaciations, both of which were capable of covering large land areas in a short time, such as occurred most recently during the Pleistocene epoch that impacted Europe and North America so profoundly.

In Canada, we are familiar with cold weather and flooding. Our country's present land area was almost completely submerged beneath thick ice only thirty-five hundred to four thousand years ago. At the same time, northern and central Europe were mantled with southward flowing glaciers. Near Okotoks, Alberta, there is a giant glacial erratic called the "Big Rock," consisting of Lower Cambrian quartzite carried by both the mountain and continental glaciers hundreds of miles from its source in the Rocky Mountains far to the south on the Western prairie grasslands. How incredible must have been these giant 'rivers' and 'floods' of moving ice!

Some of Job's later contemporaries encountered terrifying climatic extremes in the Northern Hemisphere associated with the Pleistocene glaciation. About 1700 kilometers north of the Land of Uz lay the continental ice sheet covering much of Eastern Europe. Large mountain glaciers buried the Alps sculpturing the folded nappes into sharp peaks like the Swiss Matterhorn and Mont Blanc. Influences of these ice sheets were felt far beyond their actual locations and were recorded in the Word of God. Man, animal life and vegetation belts migrated south as the Arctic conditions expanded.

God is in complete control of the earth's climate patterns and weather events. God sends the cold and glaciers as well as rain and floods. We have heard of historical battles in which a weather event played the vital role in defeat for one side and victory for another. Two cases are Hitler's and Napoleon's armies who met their doom in unusually cold Russian winters. God sent that cold to perform his will geo-politically. The British Expeditionary Force was spared destruction at Dunkirk in June, 1940, by an unusually thick and prolonged maritime fog. There are numerous examples of this kind mentioned in human history. Noah's Flood was a horrible judgment causing the near extinction of the human race, except for 8 people. That shows how serious sin is to a Holy God.

Biblical references do not mention the word 'glaciation' because it is a relatively new term in the English language. There are, however, statements that speak of the existence of very significant amounts of snow and ice in the Book of Job and in the Psalms. They are consistent with the same type of verses from which we interpret continental drift and orogeny. Two examples are Job 38:22-23 and 29 where God is speaking to Job in the same context as in the description of ***"behemoth"*** in Chapter 6.

> *"Hast thou entered into the treasures of the snow? or hast thou seen the treasures of the hail, Which I have reserved against the time of trouble, against the day of battle and war? Out of whose womb came the ice? and the hoary frost of heaven, who hath gendered it?"*

Witnessing a Pleistocene glaciation from afar would be a terrifying experience, if one survived. God asks Job in verse 22 if he has entered into the *"treasures of the snow."* The question is asked because Job has not entered in. *"Treasures"* signify large accumulations of snow as a treasure of any kind would, money or gold. To have *"entered into"* such an event would mean certain death. No man would want to enter into God's treasures of snow. Even today glaciers are forbidding places because a large amount of snow accumulation is necessary for the ice to form. Whiteouts are common. In verse 29, *"ice"* is described as coming forth *"out of whose womb?"* A womb is the place of birth, out of which comes a baby human being or animal. It is associated with a sudden release of waters followed quickly by the actual newborn. Job 38:8 illustrates this principle,

> *"Or who shut up the sea with doors, when it brake forth, as if it had issued out of the womb?"*

Scripture, therefore, uses the *"womb"* figuratively to illustrate the sudden release of ice from its place of 'birth,' meaning the center of accumulation of a glacier. Verse 29 continues to develop this thought. It describes the cold associated with frost and snow and uses the term *"gendered"* (give birth to) in relation to the womb and ice. The context of Job 38:22 and 29 makes it clear that snow and ice comes from God and that He can send it in large amounts like water and a newborn baby from the womb. This sudden breaking forth of cold, snow and ice is describing conditions of glaciation known to Job's generation. A profound climate change creating huge snowfall and a rapid burial by glaciers would affect human beings dramatically. Ice would flow out of the high mountainous, temperate and polar climates like water breaking out of the womb, suddenly and inexorably destroying everything in its path. Witnessed by man, it would be a momentous event and certain to be recorded in Scripture as the other natural physical phenomena.

> *"God thundereth marvelously with his voice; great things doeth he, which we cannot comprehend. For he saith to the snow, Be thou on the earth; likewise to the small rain, and to the great rain of his strength."* (Job 37:5-6)

The Book of Job speaks of snow and ice in context to *"great things"* happening *"which we cannot comprehend."* Among these incomprehensible things is great rain; and snow follows in the same logical trend. Great snow would cause the necessary accumulations needed for glaciers to develop. Witnessing ice lobes breaking out of the womb of the north and covering the land surface would be difficult for man to comprehend. We would respond in a similar way today if a wall of ice plowed out of the north at more than 40 miles per year and wiped out the cities of Calgary and Edmonton. It would demonstrate the power and judgment of God. Thousands of feet of ice would grind almost everything below it to powder.

Psalm 147:16-17 gives the sense of intense cold accompanying glacial conditions and the formidable obstacle it presented to men living in the northern parts of Europe and North America. Native creation stories speak of a growing wall of ice to the north.

> *"He giveth snow like wool: he scattereth the hoarfrost like ashes. He casteth forth his ice like morsels: who can stand before his cold?"*

> "That time frame also accords with native creation stories cited by Dewar that speak of a growing wall of ice to the North, suggesting a human presence in the Americas before the last ice age." (Bethune, B., March 19, 2001, MacLean's Magazine)

Giving snow like *"wool"* and *"ashes"* again suggests significant amounts. Casting forth ice is not speaking of hail but of snow associated with intense cold. The Psalmist asks, *"who can stand before his cold?"* The obvious answer, in context, means 'no one.' The modern Inuit could stand before cold Arctic weather and survive the long winter's freezing temperatures for many generations. But no one could stand before God's cold when He cast forth His ice like morsels, wool and ashes. This statement means there were times in the past when no living being could endure God's snow and ice. They had to flee, if they could, or die.

My Uncle George gave me the following testimony concerning the arctic cold. In the early 1960s he was working on the DEW (Distant Early Warning) Line in northern Manitoba, Canada. He and a colleague were out on a very cold and windy winter day. He exited the vehicle in which they were driving, wearing a warm winter parka with a hood and snout covering his nose and mouth. He pulled back the hood for a moment to breath but the extreme cold caused him to gasp and draw the cold air into his lungs. He collapsed with the shock and froze one of his lungs, almost instantly. After that he could no longer work and needed bottled oxygen to breathe properly.

The Polar regions have had in the past far colder conditions than my uncle experienced. Woolly Mammoths have been found frozen in the Alaskan and Siberian permafrost with undigested grasses in their mouths, their flesh still edible as if they had been 'flash frozen.' A 'quick freeze' had occurred that even these resilient Arctic creatures could not withstand. Pastor John Linton wrote an account concerning such discoveries in "The Flood of Noah's Day," (date unspecified). This terrifying scene pictures the kind of snow and cold described in the Scriptures. Both men and animals succumbed to the power of God's cold.

> "In Siberia, where the ground is frozen to a great depth, the animals were frozen as they were engulfed, so that their hair, skin and flesh are as fresh today as on the day they died; and the distension of the nostrils, and the gorging of the blood vessels of the head with coagulated blood, proves that they died from suffocation. Extinct animals, such as the mammoth, and the woolly rhinoceros, with lions, oxen, deer, man and even birds, pack some of the caves from the floor to the ceiling; they are found huddled together in the wildest confusion; no bones are gnawed, showing that overmastering terror tamed the fiercest, and that they did not perish from each

other's fangs; and in some caves their heads are found in every case turned toward the north."

*"Out of the south cometh the whirlwind: and cold out of the north."* (Job 37:9)

Man experienced overwhelming cold coming out of the north, the direction associated with the bulk of the Pleistocene ice advance that engulfed much of the Northern Hemisphere. The above excerpt is an example and the following Scripture confirms this fact. Evolutionists teach that 'Stone Age' man lived during the last 'Ice Age'. There is no such thing as stone-age humans. Job and his contemporaries were far from being uncivilized savages. On average, they were much smarter than we are. And they lived contemporaneous with the dinosaurs. Where is the 'stone age?' It's only in men's minds! Those with the hard heads.

Freezing also extended to the oceanic areas in the northern and southern polar latitudes.

*"The waters are hid as with a stone, and the face of the deep is frozen."* (Job 38:22, 29-30)

In Scripture, the *"face of the deep"* normally refers to seas or oceans, large bodies of water that were challenging obstacles to man's movement. The Arctic Ocean today is nearly impassable to surface ships in winter due to a thick layer of ice, although that is slowly changing. But during the Pleistocene ice age it was an open ocean as seawater was necessary to generate the moisture required for glaciation of much of the Northern Hemisphere.

Glaciation was followed by periods during which the climate ameliorated and the glaciers melted. Immediately following the Scriptural description of abundant snow, ice and irresistible cold is a verse stating that these mild conditions and melting could come with equal suddenness.

*"He sendeth out his word, and melteth them: he causeth his wind to blow, and the waters flow."* (Psalm 147:17)

*"He sendeth forth his commandment upon earth: his word runneth very swiftly."* (Psalm 147:15)

The patriarchs, including Job, knew about catastrophes involving water, snow and ice. There is ample evidence from the inspired writings for the physical processes involved in glaciation. It agrees with the Scriptures describing continental breakup, seafloor spreading, orogenic deformation and dinosaurs.

But what specifically caused the Pleistocene and earlier ice ages?

"Some unknown factor," writes Zeuner, "created conditions favourable for glaciation during the Pleistocene." (Holmes, A., 1964, Principles of Physical Geology, p. 705).

The starting point for recognizing the cause of Pleistocene glaciation is Biblical chronology and the processes that were operative during "the days of Peleg." As a time of catastrophic, non-uniformitarian earth processes, it played a vital role in later Pleistocene glaciation. Noah's Flood provided the same conditions for the earlier Precambrian and Paleozoic 'ice ages'. The Pleistocene occurred after the completion of most of the physical displacements associated with rapid seafloor spreading and continental drift. These crustal movements influenced both snowfall and its accumulation far beyond the normal limits. How did this happen?

Both the Late Tertiary orogeny and the Pleistocene glaciation are constrained by Biblical chronology leaving little time for one to grade into the other. Therefore, the 'ice age' must have begun almost instantaneously, possibly in only a few decades. Let us examine how this could have happened.

The key to understanding sudden Pleistocene glaciation lies in synthesizing continental drift, seafloor spreading, volcanism and orogeny within the Biblical time frame. The ice advance in the Northern Hemisphere correlates with the end of the worldwide Tertiary orogenic cycle **(Figure 5**, p. 31**)**. As the earth was being divided continental plates collided and huge volumes of volcanic lava were extruded over a very short period. These eruptions dwarfed modern examples such as Krakatoa and Mount St. Helens, and were worldwide in extent. They spewed out dark clouds of ash causing a significant cooling of the atmosphere globally. Also, submarine extrusion of basaltic lava continued to produce new seafloor beneath the opening ocean basins until *"the earth was divided"* at the end of the "days of Peleg." Rapid creation of oceanic crust warmed the oceans' waters worldwide.

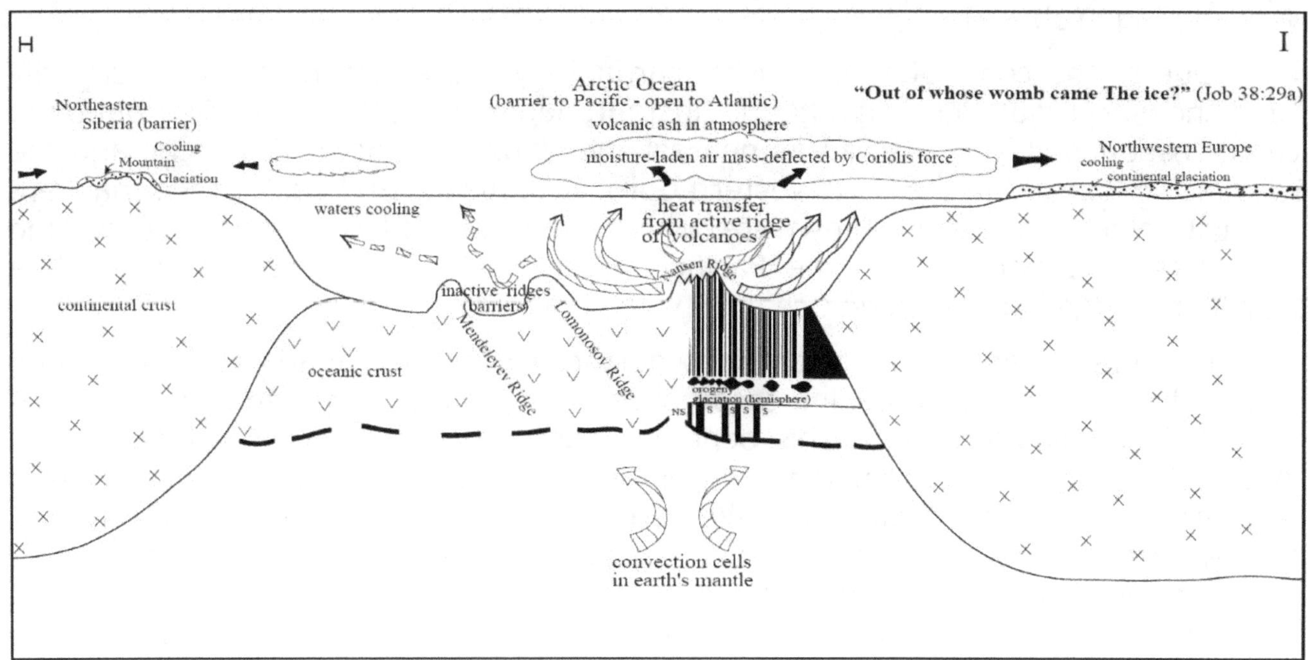


**Figure 14**

The interpreted mechanism for Pleistocene glaciation according to the Biblical chronology. Rapid seafloor spreading generates humid air masses that spread over the adjacent continents. They release massive amounts of snow due to atmospheric cooling caused by large concentrations of ash from Tertiary volcanoes in worldwide mountain belts.

The movement of large landmasses into the northern latitudes set the stage for Pleistocene glaciation. Laurasia and Gondwana broke up and the Atlantic Ocean opened at a rate of at least 10 to 15 miles per year. Fragments of the Laurasian super-continent drifted into northern waters and restricted what had previously been an open ocean **(Figure 12b)**. At the same time, high rates of spreading elevated the interiors of the continents while depressing their margins. As the northern landmasses converged upon the Arctic Ocean Tertiary basalt seafloor was first generated along the Mendeleyev Ridge; then it was abandoned and became inactive. Then spreading followed the Lomonosov Ridge, which in turn became inactive and abandoned. Finally, seafloor spreading moved eastward forming the Nansen Ridge, contiguous with the Mid-Atlantic Ridge. It acted as a 'heat engine' providing the source of warm, upwelling waters for generating atmospheric moisture in the northern latitudes. Marine convection currents emanated from the upwelling seafloor transferring massive amounts of water vapor into the overlying atmosphere of the semi-restricted Arctic Ocean, surrounded by the converging continents of Eurasia and North America. Combined with atmospheric cooling caused by intense Tertiary volcanism, moisture-laden air masses formed over the cooling ocean and overrode the adjacent continents. Massive weather systems formed intense, high-pressure super-storm cells that moved southward over the cooler landmasses releasing huge amounts of snow. **Figure 13** depicts this mechanism in a cross-section profile. The magnetic stripes form a mirror-image on both sides of the Nansen Ridge (above).

Due to the constraints of Biblical chronology these factors caused incredibly rapid snow accumulation and a nearly 'instantaneous glaciation.' The distribution of ice corresponds closely with areas nearest the Nansen Ridge in the Arctic and the East Pacific Rise along the northwestern Cordillera. Alaska and eastern Siberia were largely unglaciated because they were further from these sources of warm upwelling seawaters, and barred from the Pacific by the Bering land bridge and inactive submarine ridges in the Arctic Ocean.

Glaciers advanced southward into northern Eurasia, Canada and the United States at velocities far exceeding those of modern ice lobes; possibly as rapidly as forty to fifty miles in a year. This behavior was due primarily to the high rate of snow build up in the accumulation centers in the northern Canadian Shield and in newly-formed mountains along the Western Cordillera. Ice built up so quickly that it accelerated the downstream parts of the glacier by pressure alone. The same thing can be demonstrated by pouring thick pancake batter on a surface and watching it flow out radially from the center of accumulation. The thicker the viscous mass the faster the flow. The 'flash freeze' and sudden inundation overwhelmed twelve million square miles of the Northern Hemisphere so rapidly that Tertiary deposition and erosion changed with sudden ferocity to the Pleistocene 'ice age' in the northernmost land areas.

So sudden was the onset of the northern cold and glaciation that wood from Early Tertiary subtropical forests is preserved unaltered at the ground surface on

Axel Heiberg Island. This recent discovery is a natural result of the Biblical chronology based upon the "days of Peleg." It cannot be explained by any other means. Secular scientists avoid facing the implications of such discoveries; for if they do, they will have to face the fact that evolution is not true; and Biblical creation is true. Therefore, we are accountable to God, our Creator; "and, for many people, that is a no-go zone." (Catchpoole, D., 2014, Evolution's Achilles' Heels)

> "Canadian scientists have announced the "stunning" discovery of a 45 million-year-old mummified forest about 1100 km from the North Pole. The site was first spotted by helicopter pilot Paul Tudge in 1985. Dr. James Bassinger called the site on Axel Heiberg Island "the world's finest known fossil forest. It's amazing preservation. The freshness of their appearance makes it look as if someone went in and logged the area last year. In places you can reach down to the ground and dig out mats of leaves. These leaves look very fresh, like you've just plucked them off the tree," he said. The scientists do not yet know why the wood was so well preserved, but they are studying such factors as climate." (Calgary Herald, 1985 "World's 'finest known fossil forest' unearthed")

The reason that the wood is so well preserved includes ***both time and climate***. It lies in a cold climate and has not been there that long. The forest was growing only about four thousand and fifty years ago on a landmass that had drifted into the extreme north at the onset of the Pleistocene glaciation. It escaped the actual ice scouring and remained essentially *in situ* (in place) when it 'died.' Like the well-preserved mammoths, these trees and their leaves were flash frozen at 'ground zero' as the Tertiary epoch changed suddenly into the Pleistocene epoch. God has allowed the discovery of these specimens to support the Biblical chronology and a young age for the earth as foretold in His Word. Only spiritual blindness can explain man's response to these amazing discoveries. It's the Darwinian paradigm in real life, folks.

> "In the more northern parts of the country (northern Siberia), large numbers of mammoths have been preserved. A large number of carcasses have been unearthed in an upright, standing position, as if they had sunk down and been frozen in that position...by a very great catastrophe...that killed the animals and buried them under continuous beds of loam and gravel, (while) a great and sudden change in climate froze the animal flesh under the ground. The remains of their last meal, consisting of elephant grass and other semi-tropical plants now foreign to that region, have been found in their stomachs. Other animals, such as rhinoceros, oxen and sheep have also been found frozen in the earth of Siberia." (Dr. Blick, E., 1986, Creation and Noah's Ark, Southwest Radio Church booklet, p. 18)

So much for the peer-imposed consensus for 'man-made' global warming. God is in control of this earth through natural and supernatural processes which are in His hand. Man's rejection of Genesis 1:1 is a fatal mistake. It leads to blanket unbelief for the rest of the Book.

As many as five cycles of glaciation occurred in the Pleistocene over a period of about five hundred years, beginning near the end of "the days of Peleg." Cyclical patterns of glacial advances and retreats were due to a complex interplay between the rates of seafloor spreading, variations in oceanic currents in the Atlantic and Pacific oceans, orogeny and the intensity of volcanism. It would be interesting to try and compare the latest Tertiary magnetic stripes with the earliest Pleistocene glacial-interglacial cycle to see if there is a correlation between the rate of seafloor spreading and the 'ice age.'

Will there be another worldwide continental glaciation? Not likely, because the requisite conditions ended more than thirty-five hundred years ago and a more stabilized climate has existed since then. The earth's 'heat engine' has decayed by 'geologic entropy' and the Arctic Ocean is now frozen, or nearly so. Because glaciers are an integral part of God's judgment, they occurred repeatedly during the Flood 'Year' and in the period immediately afterward. The Pleistocene was the last active geological phase at the end of, or immediately following, "the days of Peleg." The Bible does not mention a future judgment by water or another accelerated phase of continental drift and volcanism, both of which would be necessary conditions for a new 'ice age.' Instead, the next judgment will be by fire when God brings the Great Tribulation to end Gentile domination over Israel and Jerusalem. As I review this passage before sending it to publication Hamas is raining rockets down on Israel. We are rapidly approaching another great judgment as man continues to ignore God's call to repentance and openly rebels against his Creator. The Biblical chronology is a strong warning to those who have dismissed God and His Word in these 'last days." He is in control, not us.

*"They that observe lying vanities forsake their own mercy."* (Jonah 2:8)

# CHAPTER 8

## THE BOOK OF JOB AND THE MIGRATION OF MAN

One of the great puzzles of secular science is the distribution of the human race in different parts of the world. There is a controversy over timing and migration paths particularly between the Eastern and the Western Hemispheres. When did man arrive in the New World and how did he get there? Asiatic people migrated to North America via the ice-free Bering land bridge according to college textbooks. But there was no passage through the glaciated Coast Mountains of British Columbia for representatives of these groups during the Pleistocene. They arrived after the last glaciation. The presence of earlier non-Asiatic peoples in the Western Hemisphere has long intrigued some secular archeologists and anthropologists. Instead of an Asiatic land bridge researchers should start to look for African and European 'land bridges,' but to do that they will have to turn to Continental Drift as viewed through the lens of Biblical chronology.

The Bible will help give us the answers to these questions, but first we must go back to the period of Noah's Flood dated at 2348 B.C. (1656 A.C.). The Flood destroyed all human beings except for eight people who heeded God's warning. Only Noah and his three sons; Shem, Ham and Japheth survived together with their wives in the ark. Emerging into the New World, they began to multiply and increased rapidly in population after leaving the ark. Modern geography would place our common ancestors, Noah's descendants, in east central Persia, possibly on a stable block of continental crust. They moved out from the "mountains of Ararat" (Genesis 8:4) in northeastern Turkey to the **east** because the Tethys Sea and its remnants occupied the Fertile Crescent of modern day Iraq. As the sea receded they moved to the west where they began to build Babel in the valley of the Tigris and Euphrates rivers. Other descendants of Noah may have migrated southward from Ararat directly to elevated parts of the stable Arabian Shield. That is the setting for the Book of Job, a near descendent of Shem.

> *"And it came to pass, as they journeyed from the east, that they found a plain in the land of Shinar; and they dwelt there."* (Genesis 11:1)

There is also a secular theory of man's movement over the earth.

> "The European and native variants diverged from a common ancestor, some geneticists argue up to 36,000 years ago." (Bethune, B., March 19, 2001, MacLean's Magazine)

More recently, Christopher Rupe and John Sanford describe it in Chapter 14 in their book, *"Contested Bones"* (2017). The popular "Out-of-Africa" model involves modern man being involved in a near-extinction event (a "genetic bottleneck") about 200,000 years ago, from which the 'Adam & Eve' genetic lineages suddenly recovered and very rapidly spread throughout the world. Modern genetics points to eastern Africa as the original source for the human gene pool that can be traced around the world in all peoples to this day. This is not inconsistent with Scripture because Babel and its early inhabitants were part of the present day Middle Eastern portion of the former supercontinent, Pangaea. The pan-African portion of this great landmass was called Gondwanaland, and the northern part, Laurasia. Rupe and Sanford also describe the biblical model as "Out-of-Middle-East" model for mankind's dispersion around the world. It agrees closely with the secular model except for the evolutionary time scale required by Darwinists for their ape-to-man paradigm.

> "humanity begins with Adam and Eve, whose descendants rapidly multiply, and then, went through a one-generation bottleneck at the time of the Flood, and then the population once again increased, followed by rapid divergence at the Tower of Babel event, creating today's people groups. Some isolated post-Babel people groups (Hobbit, Naledi, Erectus, Neanderthal, etc.) became compromised due to inbreeding. With the advent of genome sequencing the evolutionary model underwent a drastic revision to accommodate the mounting genetic data. Remarkably, the biblical model is already in agreement with the latest genetic data, no revisions necessary." (Rupe, C., and Sanford, J., 2017, Contested Bones, p.345)

If we were to find fossil bones of the earliest Post-Flood humans they would be *Homo sapiens* just like us. Darwin's early 'progenitor' of the human race has been found fraudulent and wrong every time with respect to being the missing link(s). There is no ape-to-man evolution. There were no 'stone-age,' semi-human beings before the Flood, nor after it. Even the time-honored cave dweller, "Neanderthal Man," now is attributed by paleontologists to have –

> "buried their dead with their heads pointing toward the sunrise, made musical instruments, had control of fire, searched the landscape for rare minerals to make cosmetics and inter-married with 'modern' man. Five or six recent genome studies show Neanderthal Man was just a family group of the same species as modern man that lived in Europe and Asia after the Flood. Neanderthal skeletons are supposedly tens of thousands of years old, yet we are still finding DNA in them. As a geneticist, that's not supposed to be; that's shocking." (Carter, R., 2014, Evolution's Achilles' Heels)

> "The failure of paleo-experts to find a legitimate "ape-like" ancestor to man over 150 years of fossil hunting is truly remarkable. This flies directly in the face of the claim that human evolution is an uncontested fact. It is clear that neither *Habilis*, nor *Sediba*, nor *Naledi* bridge the vast evolutionary gap between the ape-like australopiths and man. Naledi appears to be a degenerate human population that lived in isolation. The missing link is still missing." (Rupe, C., and Sanford, J., 2017, Contested Bones, pp. 230-231)

> "*Australopithecus* bones are commonly found with human *(Homo)* fossils and artifacts in the very same bone bed. These observations are routinely dismissed because ancestors and descendants should not typically live simultaneously in the same niche, and because the *Homo* bones and artifacts are showing up long before

the genus *Homo* is said to have evolved. There is no critical bridge species between *Australopithecus* and *Homo*...When there are nearly complete skeletons there is no ambiguity – the bones can be readily identified as either *Australopithecus* (extinct ape genus) or *Homo* (modern man)...All ape types have historically coexisted with man, as did the australopiths before they went extinct." (Ibid, pp. 332, 334)

The antediluvian civilization was highly advanced, but all evidence of it was wiped out by Noah's Flood. There are no human fossils from the Pre-Flood world. Usher's dates give an estimated time for Lamech's generation of about 3,500 to 3,800 B.C. Six generations after Creation on the line of Adam's son, Cain, the Bible says,

*"And Lamech took unto him two wives: the name of the one was Adah, and the name of the other Zillah. And Adah bare Jabal: he was the father of such as dwell in tents, and of such as have cattle. And his brother's name was Jubal: he was the father of all such as handle the harp and organ. And Zillah, she also bare Tubal-cain, an instructor of every artificer in brass and iron: and the sister of Tubal-cain was Naamah."* (Genesis 4:19-22)

The Flood and the reason for it are given in the Book of Job Chapter 22, verses 15 to 17. The world's condition then sounds the same as today. The Post-Flood drying of the earth is also mentioned.

*"Hast thou marked the old way which wicked men have trodden? Which were cut down out of time, whose foundation was overflown by a flood: Which said unto God, Depart from us: and what can the Almighty do for them?"*

*"The flood breaketh out from the inhabitant; even the waters forgotten of the foot: they are dried up, they are gone away from men."* (Job 28:4)

God commanded Noah's descendants to spread abroad and replenish the earth but they were unwilling to comply. Their rebellion found expression at the Tower of Babel where man again began to challenge God's authority and do his own will. They progressed with amazing but satanic efficiency. The Lord intervened, confused their language and scattered them over the entire globe to save mankind from again destroying himself. Therefore, all modern nations and languages originated from eight people who initially multiplied in the Middle East, migrated to Babel, and from there were scattered to the far reaches of the globe.

*"And the LORD said, Behold, the people is one, and they have all one language; and this they begin to do: and now nothing will be restrained from them, which they have imagined to do. Go to, let us go down, and there confound their language, that they may not understand one another's speech. So the LORD scattered them abroad from thence upon the face of all the earth: and they left off to build the city."* (Genesis 11:6-8)

The Post-Flood dividing of the earth and all the related geological phenomena were a consequence of God dealing mercifully with man to scatter him and create natural and linguistic barriers to prevent the human race from uniting in another rebellion against God. In this way God was able to seek and to save men rather than to destroy all humanity.

> *"O the depth of the riches both of the wisdom and knowledge of God! how unsearchable are his judgments, and his ways past finding out!* (Romans 11:33)

In 2021, mankind is again approaching a crisis-point where God's soon intervention is inevitable. The human race is in full worldwide rebellion against God, claiming even to be able to control the earth's climate.

Living creatures from off the ark spread out through Pangaea before Noah's descendants were dispersed from Babel. They were already established in the New World by then so that a source of food would be ready for migrating man upon his arrival there. That explains why land animals and fowl of all kinds are found throughout the Eastern and Western Hemispheres. Darwin found a remarkable similarity in species worldwide and noted that repeatedly in his *On the Origin of Species (1859)*. They could not have crossed the Atlantic Ocean unless they had reached the Americas before the earth "was divided" during Peleg's days. Dinosaur fossils are found in Mesozoic sedimentary rocks in many parts of North and South America. Alberta contains some of the richest dinosaur fossil beds in Cretaceous sandstones and shales.

The missing link to the human puzzle confronting modern archeology is the Scriptural evidence of the dispersion from Babel, and the dividing of the earth in the "days of Peleg." The Bible indicates that mankind spread out from a central point to ultimately inhabit the earth. Their movement was probably radial approximating the spokes of a wheel. The shortest distance from Babel to Monte Verde, Chile, is not across Asia and down the axis of North and South America, a distance of over 25,000 kilometers. A more plausible explanation is that man came 6000-to-8000 kilometers from the east, across northern Gondwanaland to the area of the present day African Bight, and then entered what is now the country of Brazil in northeastern South America. Because the South Atlantic Ocean formed later than (i.e.: in the Lower Cretaceous) the Central Atlantic Ocean, and shallow seas were less prevalent, the descendants of Ham were able to reach points west before the time of full rupture. They probably occupied what is now the Guyana Shield and the Lower Amazon basin and spread out from there. Their ancestors would have reached modern day Central America and the Texas Gulf Coast area.

Bipedal human footprints occur together with sauropod dinosaur tracks in the Lower Cretaceous Glen Rose Fm. limestone along the Paluxy River in Texas. The footprints are not 'carved' frauds, but depress the sedimentary laminations under them showing they formed while the sediments were still soft (Ray Strom, personal communication). Sadly, creationists seem to have soft-peddled this find because it is so "problematic" to the prevailing Darwinian narrative. They should not have done this. Face the facts and try to figure them out using the Biblical chronology. This finding is considered to be totally unacceptable to the scientific establishment, but it has never been proved false. So man entered the Americas at least during Upper

Jurassic or Lower Cretaceous time, after the land animals had already begun to populate these regions.

As men progressively spread out and away from Babel after the confusion of languages, they were 'caught' in the series of events accompanying the breakup of Pangea. First was the upward swelling of the earth's crust and the formation of an extensive system of rift valleys, similar in character to the younger East African Rift System of today. At least one hundred of these rift valleys or graben developed along the fracture zone that spawned the Atlantic Ocean. Earthquakes and rapid sedimentation in rivers and lakes within these graben would have forced the early travelers to move out and away from sites of rupturing into quieter areas on opposite sides of the newly-forming Atlantic. Some of the rifts accumulated evaporitic salt deposits which suggest that they were in a hot, arid climate that would be inhospitable to human habitation and a barrier to travel. The rapidity of the seafloor spreading produced an ever widening and deepening ocean which prevented the migrants from returning to their ancestral homeland. Some people were trapped on the American side of the chasm, and others on the African/European side as basaltic crust upwelled and spread outward from the Mid-Atlantic Ridge. It appears that descendants of Japheth reached North America prior to the opening of the Central Atlantic and shallow seas further to the north. Descendants of Ham spread out across northern Gondwanaland which had no major barriers and was at equatorial latitudes. They would have reached the reached the area of the later African 'Bight'/Amazon Basin before it ruptured to form the South Atlantic Ocean, which opened in 'scissor-fashion' from south to north. The inhabitants of Monte Verde, Chile, are not among the earliest of these inhabitants, but they do record later human migration patterns following the latest Tertiary catastrophic upheavals that formed today's Andes Mountains.

This progression of events helps to explain the similarities between some of the Middle American cultures (i.e., Incas, Aztecs and Mayas) and the early advanced civilizations along the Nile River of Africa (i.e., Egypt). The Biblical evidence suggests that man first travelled to the Americas overland from Europe and North Africa and not across the Bering 'land bridge' as theorized by modern scholars. Recent findings of ancient artifacts and human remains in Southern Chile have exploded the concept that man migrated to the Middle Americas via Siberia and Alaska.

> "The Americas were inhabited by human beings...far earlier and half a world farther south than previously believed, a team of nine archeologists reports....That suggests that the first Asian immigrants arrived by a different path than the one traditionally assumed (across what is now the Bering Strait) or got there much earlier than the current scientific consensus allows, or both....'It totally changes how we think of the prehistory of America,' said Monte Verde team member Dennis Stanford of the Smithsonian Institution....the work was 'a kind of paradigm buster' and 'a new benchmark in knowledge.'...At a minimum, the new find will oblige scholars to reconsider the standard explanation of what Dillehay called "the first

chapter of human history in the Americas." (The Calgary Herald, February 15, 1997)

"Brazilian anthropologist Walter Neves maintains that the skull of Luzia, whose remains, found in Lapa Vermelha in southern Brazil, are the hemisphere's oldest, and have..."fine African features." The sheer number of Clovis sites in the southeastern United States, far from the route to South America envisioned in the Clovis model (i.e., Asia) — has long intrigued scientists. A researcher at the respected Smithsonian Institution recently came up with a startling solution. Noting that Clovis spear points have not been found in Alaska or Siberia—as would be expected by the Bering land-bridge theory — and that the Solutrean culture that flourished in Spain and France thousands of years earlier did produce similar artifacts, Dennis Stanford sees Clovis' origins in Europe. But most experts find the so-called Atlantic crossing scenario over an ice-choked ocean in some sort of skin-and-wood boat, preposterous." (Bethune, B., March 19, 2001, in MacLean's Magazine).

The latest date for the dispersion from Babel is estimated to have taken place during the early part of the "days of Peleg," about one hundred to one hundred and fifty years after the Flood **(Figures 2b and 5,** recopied from page 31, see below**)**. Human history on land could have begun even earlier because bipedal human-like footprints have been identified by Jerry MacDonald in Lower Permian beds in the Robledos Mountains of southern New Mexico (Ray Strom, personal communication). Using the Biblical history of Noah's Flood as a starting point and the "days of Peleg" as the full break-up of Pangaea, man and the animals could have left the ark even as early as the Middle-to-Upper Paleozoic time in secular terminology, reaching as far as Texas and New Mexico by the late Paleozoic and early Mesozoic (Ibid). The earth's population was probably several tens of thousands by that time; enough people from which the many languages and dialects found in the world today developed. There are currently about 6,300 known languages worldwide. The descendants of Noah's son, Japheth, arrived in Europe and North America *before* Pangaea had completely broken up, and *before* the Pleistocene 'ice age' **(Figure 12)**. Japheth was the most widely dispersed of Noah's three sons. Genesis 9:27a states:

*"God shall enlarge Japheth, and he shall dwell in the tents of Shem;"*

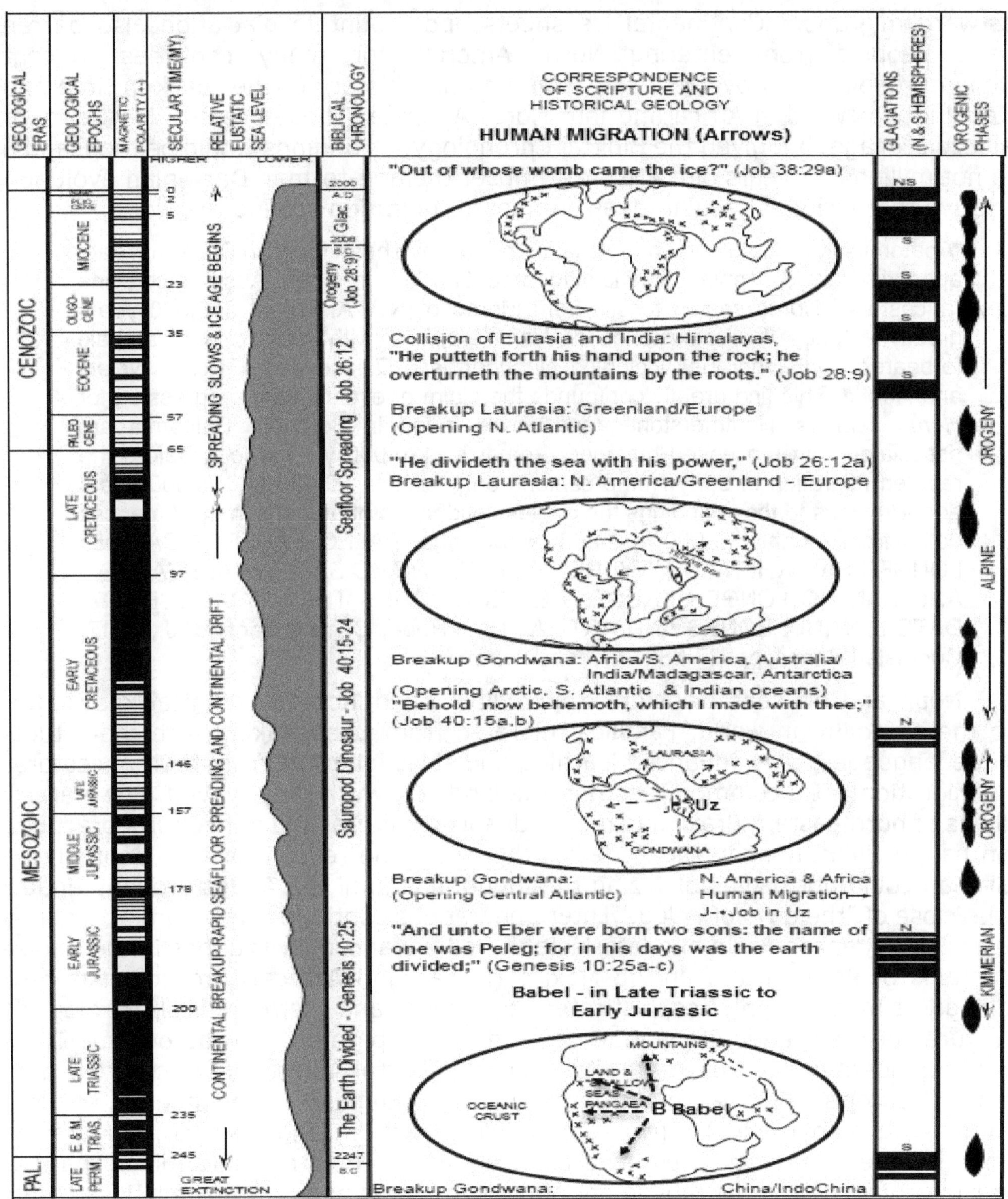


**Figure 5** (recopied from page 31)

Biblical chronology thus allows man to first populate all of the continents without any critical barriers such as wide oceans and young, high mountain ranges. The formation of large and sometimes impassable, expanses of ocean impeded later westward migration. Continental ice sheets and mountain glaciation also barred Asiatic peoples from entering North America for many centuries. Recent paleoanthropology discoveries are pushing human history further back in time and extending westward in Africa and into North America. These are not 'Mesozoic' or 'Paleozoic' in age, but given the Biblical Chronology, all findings would be thousands, and not millions, of years old. AND, they upset the ape-to-man Darwinian evolution narrative that includes secular ideas on human migration around the world.

> "Anatomically modern human-looking footprints have been found in Crete that date approximately 5.7 mya, significantly predating our reputed Australopithecine "ancestors." *Homo sapien* fossils from Morocco (NW Africa) at 315,000 years greatly extends the coexistence of *Homo sapiens* with their reputed archaic forbearers/contemporaries including *Neanderthals, Denisovans, Erectus, Naledi* and *Hobbit.* This find greatly confounds the claim of evolutionary progression for *Homo sapiens.* Hammerstones and anvils found in Southern California are associated with processed mastodon remains (130,000 yrs.) is long before the reputed migration of early *Homo sapiens* out of Africa 50,000 to 100,000 years ago. Previous to these findings the earliest evidences of humans in the Americas dates from roughly 12,000 to 14,000 years ago. PALEO EXPERTS CAN NO LONGER SAY WHEN AND WHERE THE FIRST *HOMO SAPIENS* APPEARED – AND CAN NO LONGER TRUST THE TECHNIQUES THEY HAVE USED TO DATE HOMININ BONES AND ARTIFACTS." (Rupe, C., and Sanford, J., 2017, Contested Bones, pp. 27-28).

Noah and his sons transferred incredible scientific and technical knowledge into the antediluvian world. Families migrated from Babel taking with them their unique languages, plus advanced learning and skills inherited from their ancestors. This migration left a common record in the lands to which they moved. The Maraca Indians of northeastern Brazil had more advanced cultural and agricultural practices than native civilizations in the Andes to the west. The reason for this 'anomaly' is that man could not begin colonizing the mountains until the Andes orogeny ended at the close of "the days of Peleg." Later generations continued westward across the present day Amazon Basin and later established advanced civilizations in the Andes Mountains of Peru (Incas) and in Mexico (Mayas and Aztecs). Archeologists find strikingly similar, highly sophisticated pyramids and astronomical/astrological structures of great antiquity worldwide, and now separated by wide oceans. They have been identified in South America (Incas), Central America (Aztecs & Mayas), Western Europe (France, earthen pyramid & England, Stonehenge), Malta, Southeast Asia (pyramids), Egypt (Pharaoh's pyramids) and Iraq (Ur, ziggurats). Many of these huge structures have precisely accurate astronomical lines that tie into the equinoxes and the movement of the sun, moon and the constellations Orion and Plieides in particular. The builders were highly intelligent and had common knowledge of detailed Pythagoran geometry nearly two thousand years before the Greeks 'invented' it. Their building projects also contain huge stones that would require some of the largest modern cranes to lift. Clearly they possessed a high degree of knowledge and technical ability. All of this advanced capability came from the Pre-Flood civilization through Noah's family and was brought to these lands ***before*** the earth was fully divided and made impassible to land and sea travel. Thus we see the impact of the Biblical chronology upon human migration and the development of civilization.

The Babel migrants lived before and after Pangaea and its two main parts, Laurasia in the north and Gondwanaland in the south (i.e., "the earth"), were "divided." They witnessed the upheavals of Peleg's days, yet quickly forgot God and fell into idolatry. They began to worship the creation instead of the Creator. Job spoke about the knowledge of astronomy in his days but rejected its growing occult emphasis expressed in astrological worship. Job was a true believer in the LORD and recognized that man was again moving into idolatry in defiance of God and His authority. Evidence of sun worship is found in Neanderthal grave sites (p. 80) Job feared to follow this kind of idolatry although he knew what it was from the civilization in which he lived.

> *"If I beheld the sun when it shined, or the moon walking in brightness; And my heart hath been secretly enticed, or my mouth hath kissed my hand: This also were an iniquity to be punished by the judge: for I should have denied the God that is above."* (Job 31:26-28)

The Lord had not created these celestial bodies to be worshipped, but to bear witness of His eternal power and Godhead. The LORD speaks to Job in this context:

> *"Canst thou bind the sweet influences of Pleiades, or loose the bands of Orion? Canst thou bring forth Mazzaroth in his season? or canst thou guide Arcturus with his sons? Knowest thou the ordinances of heaven? canst thou set the dominion thereof in the earth?"* (Job 38:31-33)

Obviously God had done all of these things, and alone was to be worshipped and glorified by men. Unfortunately, man's heart is desperately wicked and sinful, and the Post-Flood descendants of Noah were no exception. They corrupted their superior knowledge and technical ability very rapidly, and decided to unite and build a city and a tower *"whose top may reach unto heaven; and let us make us a name."* Today's growing emphasis on global government and man's ability to control the earth's climate, chart his own path and solve his own problems is a repeat of this same mistake. Like Babel, it will result in God's judgment which will catastrophically end "the times of the Gentiles." (Luke 21:24)

Earth processes affected the migration of Noah's immediate descendants during the Cenozoic and Mesozoic Eras. Their initial movement out from Mt. Ararat has already been mentioned. Somewhat later, the northern part of Gondwanaland and Western Europe formed the optimum paths of migration to the 'New World.' Seafloor spreading opened the Central Atlantic Ocean earliest giving less time for migrants to reach eastern North America from Europe and northwest Africa **(Figure 5)**. Yet, they did arrive in sufficient numbers to leave a record in North America, an example being the European DNA in Canada's Ojibwa people (see below). The Atlantic Ocean would later form a 2,000 to 4,000 mile wide barrier preventing any significant westward human migration from Europe or Africa for the next thirty-five hundred years!

> "Provocative DNA studies have pointed to Asian origins for four lineages that characterize more than 95 per cent of indigenous Americans. But a fifth DNA lineage, most commonly detected in Canada's Ojibwa people, has no known Asian affiliation. It does, however, turn up in Europeans." (Bethune, B., March 19, 2001, in MacLean's Magazine)

Pleistocene ice sheets greatly impeded the growth and spread of human civilization in the Northern Hemisphere. Glaciation established harsh continental weather patterns that drastically affected life. Many of the earliest inhabitants probably died and the rest were driven far to the south. Even today it is possible to have snow storms and freezing temperatures in the southern United States during the winter months. People in Texas froze to death during one such episode in early 2021 when the power grid went down. Think how severe the storms must have been when the northern half of the continent was covered with ice! People would have required hundreds of years to colonize the glaciated areas after the final melting. Nomadic migrants of Asiatic decent came to North America across the Bering Strait after the Pleistocene glaciers receded. They mingled together with remnants of the earlier civilization and gradually became the dominant group. This trend continued until the arrival of Europeans in the fifteenth century A.D. in modern sailing ships.

The Biblical chronology shows a far different pattern of events to the south where Indian civilization was highly advanced. These South and Central American peoples had more time and fewer climatic obstacles to prevent them carrying on, and maintaining an advanced culture and technology. Architecture, urban organization and agricultural practices were highly developed, having been imported directly from Mesopotamia and Egypt. Their Hamite ancestors traversed the northern portion of the present-day African Shield, entering western Gondwana before it broke up to form Africa, South America and the South Atlantic Ocean. They crossed over in the vicinity of the African Bight, the last area to separate. Some may have sailed across the South Atlantic in its early formative stages. From there they colonized the stable platform of the Guiana Shield in northeastern Brazil **(Figure 5)**. Traces of their migration path are still found today in the northern Amazon Basin (p. 83-84)

All of these human movements tie back to Noah's Flood, the Tower of Babel, the confusion of languages and the "days of Peleg" in which the earth was divided – a period not involving the evolution of stone age people to modern man, but the migration highly intelligent and capable individuals who spread out to populate the earth by God's express command in the Book of Genesis.

> *"So the LORD scattered them abroad from thence upon the face of all the earth: and they left off to build the city. Therefore is the name of it called Babel; because the LORD did there confound the language of all the earth: and from thence did the LORD scatter them abroad upon the face of all the earth."* (Genesis 11:8-9)

# CHAPTER 9

## THE BOOK OF JOB AND DARWINISM

**Job was called *"the greatest of all the men of the east"* in Job 1:3. In Job Chapters 38 to 41, God speaks to Job out of the whirlwind and states His position as Creator and sustainer of all things living and material. Time and time again God says to Job, "I made it all, and where were you when I did it?" When God finished speaking to Job, Job spoke to God,**

***"Then the LORD answered Job out of the whirlwind, and said, Who is this that darkeneth counsel by words without knowledge? Moreover the LORD answered Job, and said, Shall he that contendeth with the Almighty instruct him? he that reproveth God, let him answer it."* (Job 38:1-2 and 40:1-2)**

***"Then Job answered the LORD, and said, I know that thou canst do everything, and that no thought can be withholden from thee. Who is he that hideth counsel without knowledge? therefore have I uttered that I understood not; things too wonderful for me, which I knew not. I have heard of thee by the hearing of the ear: but now mine eye seeth thee. Wherefore I abhor myself, and repent in dust and ashes."* (Job 42: 1-3, 5-6)**

**In contrast to Job, Charles Darwin (1809-1882), the naturalist, and author of *On the Origin of Species (1859)* achieved something very different than Job, and**

**"is widely considered one of the greatest scientists of our age, if not the greatest scientist in the entire history of humankind. Darwin is most well-known specifically for his theory of evolution." (Bergman, J., 2011, The Dark Side of Charles Darwin, p. 9)**

Charles Darwin's statue sits in highest honor in Westminster Abbey, along with that of Isaac Newton, the great God-fearing scientist and mathematician. Newton's place of eminence is richly deserved; Darwin's is not. Darwin was not a scientist. He earned a degree in Theology, and was at best only a nominal Christian in his early years. Later in his life he completely rejected the Christian faith and warred against it with the theory of evolution. Jerry Bergman's recent 270 page book, *The Dark Side of Charles Darwin* (2011) contains 928 carefully referenced writings that expose this icon of science as far different from the sanitized image presented in the media and academia. Both Newton's and Darwin's remains are interred in that famous building. In contrast to Newton, who loved and honored God, Darwin set out to "murder God," by separating man from his Maker through destroying faith in God's Word, the Bible.

> "Beyond its impact on traditional science, Darwinism was devastating to conventional theology." (Ferrell, V., The Evolution Handbook, 2001, p. 805, quote by D. Nelkin, 1977)
>
> "Milner wrote Darwin "dreamt of being beheaded or hanged" due to his theory, and once even stated that evolution was a "belief that went so contrary to biblical authority [that it] was 'like confessing a murder,'" the murder of God." (Ibid, p. 110)
>
> "Darwinism has had a devastating impact on society. Its ramifications reach into the deepest aspects of social life and culture. Evolutionary theory has had a most terrible, desolating effect on Western Civilization in the 20th century. [He who does not honor Darwin] inevitably attracts the speculative psychiatric eye to himself. It is a religion of science that Darwinism chiefly held, and holds over men's minds today." (Ferrell, V., 2001, quotes from pp. 794-800 in The Evolution Handbook, 992 pp.)
>
> "One study of 149 leading biologists found that 89.9% believed that evolution has no ultimate purpose or goal except survival, and that humans are a cosmic accident existing at the whim of time and chance. Only a mere 6% believed that evolution has a purpose beyond survival. **Most all of those who believed evolution had no purpose were hard core atheists**. Many people have concluded that there is nothing worth living for or no cause worth dying for. This reflects itself in the fact that, especially among the young, a major cause of death is suicide." (Bergman, J., 2011, The Dark Side of Charles Darwin, pp. 80-81)

Michael White opined that, for biologists today,

> "Darwin is second only to God, and for many he might rank still higher." Steven Jay Gould wrote that all early theories of origins cited God for their support, and "Darwin comes close to this status [a god] among evolutionary biologists." Admitting Darwin's own doubts and misgivings about his theory and life no doubt would detract considerably from Darwin's godlike image. **Yet he founded a religion, the secular religion of evolution that, for many, replaced the theistic religions**." (Ibid, p. 120)

Today's schools and universities are "Darwin's converts." They pay homage to Charles Darwin (1809-1882) by describing ultimate origins in context to Darwinian Theory and teaching it to their students. Who was this man whose hold on men's minds extends to the present day over much of the scientific world?

> "Charles Darwin was born into wealth and was able to have a life of ease. He took two years of medical school at Edinburgh University, and then dropped out. It was

the only scientific training he ever received. Because he spent his time in bars with his friends, he barely passed his courses. *Never a scientist*, and knowing nothing about the practicalities of genetics...he and two friends pirated and published Russell Wallace's theory of evolution under his own name...Darwin had no particular purpose in life...but an influential relative got him a position as the unpaid "naturalist" on a ship (*the HMS Beagle*) planning to sail around the world from 1831 to 1836. While a naturalist aboard the *Beagle*, Darwin was initiated into witchcraft in South America by nationals. He took part in their ceremonies and, as a result, *something happened to him.* Upon his return to England, although his health was strangely weakened, he spent the rest of his life working on theories to destroy faith in the Creator. He developed a chronic and incapacitating illness, and went to his death under a depression he could not shake." (Ferrell, V., 2001, The Evolution Handbook, pp. 24-28, 992 pp.)

From the time Darwin began working on his theory of evolution at about the age of 30 his health began to fail. He spent the rest of his life in severe physical and mental infirmity at home cared for by his devout Christian wife, Emma, and going out but little. He lost the comfort of God and His Word and had extreme fits of physical disability that doctors could not treat. The cause was believed to be psychological, due to his abandonment of God and God's abandonment of him. Therefore, his root problem was spiritual, and may very likely have been demon possession, as described in the Scriptures.

"Darwin suffered from various combinations of severe psychological (or psychologically influenced) health problems, including severe depression, fits of hysterical crying, shaking, severe anxiety, insomnia, fainting spells, muscle twitches, trembling, nausea, vomiting, personalization, visual hallucinations, malaise, vertigo, cramps, bloating and nocturnal flatulence, headaches, nervous exhaustion, dyspnea, tachycardia, tinnitus, and sensations of loss of consciousness and impending death." (Bergman, J., 2011, The Dark Side of Charles Darwin, p. 116)

*"Master (Jesus), I have brought to thee my son, which hath a dumb spirit; And wheresoever he taketh him, he teareth him; and he foameth, and gnasheth with his teeth, and pineth away: and I spake to thy disciples that they should cast him out; and they could not. And they brought him unto him (Jesus): and when he saw him, straightway the spirit tare him; and he fell on the ground, and wallowed foaming. And he asked his father, How long is it ago since this came unto him? And he said, Of a child. When Jesus saw that the people came running together, he rebuked the foul spirit, saying unto him, Thou dumb and deaf spirit, I charge thee, come out of him, and enter no more into him. And the spirit cried, and rent him sore, and came out of him: and he was as one dead; insomuch that many said, he is dead. But Jesus took him by the hand, and lifted him up; and he arose."* (Mark 9:17-18, 20-22, 25-27)

So, many of today's educated elite virtually worship a man who quit medical school after the second year, performed poorly in his classes, did not have a science background and ended his days mentally disturbed. Many of Darwin's strongest advocates would have disdained to have such a student in their own classes. They would have feared to have him in their classes. These facts alone should make modern evolutionary-minded scientists, politicians and sociologists re-think their commitment to Darwinian philosophy. Why follow the teachings of a man who would have dropped out of your classes, or only passed his courses with mediocre grades – and on top of all that – never graduated in science?? Why do you let 'his' theory have so much power over you? Something is wrong! Yet, the Darwinian 'spirit' literally possesses academia today.

The author recently read Darwin's first edition, *"On the Origin of Species,"* published in 1859. He took notes throughout that original 545 page book that on his Kindle e-reader was 212 pages. Notable was Darwin's complete ignoring of any reference to the Bible and no mention of the word, "God," anywhere in his book. He made a small number of references to the "Creator," but did not identify who the Creator was despite studying Theology at Christ's College Cambridge at a time when Christianity was strongly influential in British life. He certainly knew and was taught from the Bible the doctrine of origins. Repeatedly, throughout his treatise he focuses on questioning and attacking the idea of independent creation and design more than any other doctrine or philosophical point of view. He seemed obsessed with making this issue his crusade.

> "It is easy to hide our ignorance under such expressions as the "plan of creation," "unity of design," etc. and to think that we give an explanation when we only restate a fact." (Darwin, C., 1859, On the Origin of Species, p. 207)

His main objective was to attack and discredit the Judeo-Christian account of Creation and Intelligent Design mentioned throughout the Bible. By doing that he specifically and repeatedly attacks the real Creator, the Lord Jesus Christ the Son of God. He strongly denies catastrophism and is surely referring to Noah's Flood in context. His aim – to destroy his reader's faith in the living God, the architect of creation and redeemer of mankind and convert them to evolution. He was THE world's ultimate 'evolangelist,' "in a half century exchanging over 14,000 letters with some 1,800 correspondents, and 'just managing his voluminous mail was truly an astounding feat."' (Bergman, J., 2011, The Dark Side of Charles Darwin, p. 70)

> "The old notion of all the inhabitants of the earth having been swept away at successive periods by catastrophes, is very generally given up, even by those geologists." (Darwin, C., 1859, On the Origin of Species, p. 137)

God played no part at all in Darwin's evolutionary process. His multitudinous analogies continually question independent creation and design. Numerous times throughout the book he refers to **"my theory."** The reader can hardly escape thinking Darwin wants special recognition for some great achievement. Thorough research of his life has revealed some disturbing facts.

> "The fact is, Darwin "had a long career of taking credit: for the work of others (and) making dishonest claims about his theory." Some even argue that his major exposition of evolution, *On the Origin of Species*, was laced with hesitancies,

> contradictions, and possible prevarication. As Davies concludes, "Charles Darwin was a very secretive man with a driving ambition...Charles Darwin – British national hero, hailed as the greatest naturalist the world has ever known, the originator of one the greatest ideas of the nineteenth century – lied, cheated and plagiarized in order to be recognized as the man who discovered the theory of evolution." (Bergman, J., 2011, The Dark Side of Charles Darwin, p. 157)

Darwin's language in his first edition of *"On the Origin of Species,"* contains many flaccid statements such as, "it is highly probable," "I can see no reason to doubt," "I am far from thinking that," "we might as a general rule," "I am strongly inclined to believe/to suspect," "I must here treat the subject with extreme brevity," with many – "might," "might," "mights," etc. etc. Darwin was far from being an excellent scientist, but he was most certainly an excellent salesman. He stole Wallace's theory and sold it to Britain's intellectual scientific establishment, overthrowing creation in the process.

> "Although Charles Darwin was highly successful in popularizing the theory of organic evolution by natural selection...he was not the originator of the major parts of the theory as is commonly supposed. Yet he implied that these and other ideas were his own creation. Good evidence now exists to support the conclusion that Darwin "borrowed" – and some claim in a few places plagiarized – all or most of his "dear child" (natural selection) from other researchers, especially his own grandfather. They were not "his own brainchild," nor his child, as he claimed, but that of others which he appropriated, **often without giving them proper credit, especially Wallace, specifically his March 1858 4,000-word manuscript**...at the heart of that famous historical event lies **a deliberate and iniquitous case of intellectual theft, deceit and lies perpetuated by Charles Darwin**. (Davies') book will also argue that two of the greatest Victorian scientists (Charles Lyell and Joseph Hooker) were willing accomplices." (Ibid, pp. 156-158)

Alfred Wallace had no social status in England so the aristocratic Darwin, with Lyell and Hooker, just pushed him aside and stole his ideas, with Charles Darwin taking credit for Wallace's theory of evolution. The British establishment let it happen. In fact, it was politically approved.

Darwin's *"On the Origin of Species"* betrays his materialistic atheism, though he tried to cloak it by referring to a 'Creator.' He published the first edition of *On the Origin of Species* at the age of 50 in 1859, and later revised 75% of the book's 3000 sentences 1-to-5 times in 5 subsequent editions, the last completed in 1872 at the age of 63 years. This methodology hardly sounds like science. In fact Darwin had many scientific shortcomings. Remember, he never studied to be a scientist in the first place. Yet, he "is often regarded as one of the most highly esteemed scientists who ever lived." (Ibid, p. 181)

> "When the *Beagle* set sail he was just 22...[and] when he began collecting specimens he was an inexperienced and rather disorganized graduate in divinity. He was appointed to the position of naturalist on *HMS Beagle* more because his social status made him a suitable companion for the captain, Robert FitzRoy, than

> for his abilities as a naturalist. Darwin was his *second* choice...Darwin rarely bothered to label any specimens he collected by island because he did not think it important...when Darwin returned to England, he presented the Zoological Society with 80 mammals and 450 birds to be mounted and identified,...but lacked the expertise to do this work himself..."Darwin had great difficulty" telling the Galapagos Island finches apart and "mixed up the samples of birds collected from different islands," etc., etc.,....WHAT REMAINS IN POSTERITY'S EYES IS A SANITIZED DARWIN WHOSE CAREER SEEMS QUITE UN-DARWINIAN...THIS UNJUSTIFIED GLORIFICATION OF GENIUS MUST BE BURIED AND FOSSILIZED ALONG WITH THE DINOSAURS." (Ibid, pp. 180-182)

Some writers have said Darwin was a Christian. The few quotes below show that was extremely unlikely. Having rejected salvation through the blood atonement of Jesus Christ it is unlikely he came to repentance later. He died in 1882 at the age of 73 years having become a sedentary and sickly "hardened atheist" in his later years.

> "As he grew older Darwin grew progressively away from Christian belief." (On the Origin of Species, Introduction, 1859)

> "Charles Darwin became an evolutionist and agnostic because of his rejection of the Biblical doctrine of divine punishment." (Helton, D., 2021, Evolution: Another False Religion of Humanism)

Darwin revered Charles Lyell (1797-1875), one of the 'fathers' of uniformitarianism. His view of vast time and the geologic record was Lyellian; with immeasurable, 'eternal' ages required to bring about his concept of life evolving from primordial simplicity to complex biological life forms over hundreds of millions, or more, of years and countless generations of organic beings. He wrote that all of the multitude of biological beings that have ever inhabited earth evolved from a few primordial life forms or archetypes. He didn't know where these archetypes came from though.

Dr. Edward Blick wrote of the failure of biologists to recognize the importance of the Second Law of Thermodynamics, "a degenerative process that is one of the fundamental laws of nature." Their promotion of Darwin's Theory of Evolution to the present day violates this immutable law of Physics. Two quotes from *On the Origin of Species* follow Blick's statement.

> "There exists a universal principle of change in nature which, in the absence of intelligence supplied by any external source, is downhill, not uphill *(i.e., Devolution – Not Evolution)*. Living and non-living systems tend to wear out, rust, or break down. Useful energy is lost, disorder increases, information becomes garbled. Historically, the biologists have made little effort to apply the Second Law of Thermodynamics to their study of living organisms. In all probability this is due in large measure to their lack of study of thermodynamics in their educational backgrounds. This lack of rigor in thermodynamics shows up in their relating the mass of detailed facts of biology, not by logical thought, but by grand sweeps of the imagination (i.e. evolution). Anthony Standen, in his brilliantly amusing yet

informative book, *Science Is A Sacred Cow*, managed to deftly puncture the ego of many biologists (and probably incurred their undying wrath) with statements such as:..."*If you take a course in biology, or read any of the textbooks, you will find extremely little that can be called scientific in any scientific sense. For there is practically nothing there but descriptive facts, and facts alone do not make a science"....**Biology is one vast mass of analogies, very different from the cold, logical thinking of the physicist**.*" (Blick, E., 1986, Creation and Noah's Ark, pp. 21-22)

"**Analogy** would lead me one step further, namely, to the belief that all animals and plants have descended from some one prototype. But analogy may be a deceitful guide. *(always...BUT)* Therefore I should infer **from analogy** that probably all the beings which have ever lived on this earth have descended from some one primordial form, into which life was first breathed."

"**Distinct species present analogous variations**; and a variety of one species often assumes some of the characters of an allied species, or reverts to some of the characters of an early progenitor."

These two quotes from pages 208 and 69 of *On the Origin of Species* betray Darwin's reliance on subjective reasoning over hard scientific facts. His book is full of analogies, assumptions and speculations. Reading it is like wading through a swamp of details about a myriad of different bugs, birds, fish, animals and environments. It overwhelms and confuses the reader with analogies. Even brilliant scientists were mesmerized by Darwin's devious and convoluted reasoning. That is how he captured the scientific world in the nineteenth century, overturning their belief in biblical origins. Darwin ignored the many warnings about his theory and his own personal doubts about its veracity. Recent studies in genetics have disproved his theory.

Dr. John Sanford has studied genetic entropy (degeneration) for 13 years and made the following statements on Darwin's theory of evolutionary organization and improvement of species from "an early progenitor" over time. He discusses its impact on the human genome below, but the implication is clear. Darwin's countless generations can't exist; genetic entropy forbids it happening for humans or any other living organism. All life is moving toward extinction by genetic entropy.

"The degeneration of the information in the DNA over time (i.e., Genetic entropy) is a profound problem. Bad mutations accumulate in the human genome and a certain fraction of our bad mutations are passed on to our children... 1$^{st}$ generation: 100 additional mutations; 2$^{nd}$ generation: 200 additional mutations; etc., etc. This is a problem for the whole race. Logically, the human race should be devolving, not evolving. The human race is degenerating; the human genome is rusting out like a car. That is why we get old and die. Natural selection can't stop increasing mutations. **Genetic entropy is profound...impacting our children and grandchildren. It is absolutely lethal to genetic evolutionary theory.**" (Evolution's Achilles' Heels, 2014, Creation Ministries International)

Darwin did not call himself an atheist, or an agnostic. Nor did he declare that he believed in the God of the Bible. He knew and wrote that there were laws governing the organization and development of life. He invoked a Creator who breathed life into a few early progenitors, then attributed the vast array of life we see on earth today and in the fossil record to secondary causes, with natural selection and survival of the fittest producing new varieties, species, genera, families, classes, etc., without God. He rejected the account of creation in Genesis Chapter 1. Darwin did not, and could not, explain where his few primordial life forms came from. He did not even try. He knew nothing of genetics for it had not yet been discovered. Darwin was away over his head in trying to explain origins with the information that he possessed. He was not a scientist, or even a professional naturalist. Most other naturalists, and even geologists of his day were skeptical of his theory. He should have stayed with God's Word and worked out from there. But Darwin did not care; he had made up his mind to overthrow – to "murder," God.

In Evolution's Achilles' Heels, 2014, a number of PhD creation scientists discuss Genetics and the Origin of Life. What follows is some of what they said. Had Darwin even known the basic details of the simplest living cell, the mycoplasma, he would have recognized in it, – **information, communication and language** – that is, **DESIGN**! That simplest of cells has in it, 580,000 coded letters of DNA, and over 400 proteins arranged and organized in a specific way to control the functions of the bacterium. The origin of one such protein by chance is impossible. Moreover, RNA cannot copy itself without a protein to help it. The simplest living things need over 350 protein-based enzymes to work. Enzyme molecules, made of very precise sequences of amino acids, speed up cellular reactions by $10^{18}$ times. The probability of 10 amino acids (out of 20) in each enzyme being exact is $(350 \text{ X } 10)^{20}$; = to a 5000 digit pin, while only a 4 digit pin provides bank card security. Even "simple" mycoplasma requires lots of information, tightly-controlled and protected; that is able to be copied and fixed when an error appears – AND – all of this must be present the first time that bacterial life appears. In your body's cell the DNA has about a million breaks every day that are fixed by an exquisite repair system. RNA is even more unstable than DNA. The postulated primordial RNA soup would have equal numbers of right-and-left handed amino acids which supposedly evolved to make our body's cells which are comprised of only left-handed amino acids. Water in that "soup" would break the RNA strands faster than they could be made. So much for the "RNA world." To top it all off, this whole miraculous, cellular DNA replication and protein synthesis system is powered by the tiny **adenosine triphosphate (ATP) syntase rotary electric motor**, the power source for most of our cellular activity – one of the wonders of the universe! ATP is a complex and *reactive* molecule not found in any biotic systems; **and without it life could not exist**. Where and how did this incredible motor come from? Darwinists cannot explain where any of these miracles of cellular life came from. They beg vast periods of time but that won't work either. It would be like trying to explain that the letters and words you are reading on this page, in this book, or any other authored book, just came to be from a bottle of ink that was randomly poured out on the paper –

and the molecules of ink gradually arranged and organized themselves by chance into a logical exposition of the subject at hand. That wouldn't happen in a thousand, million or billion years without information, communication and language; and that must come from DESIGN, even in authoring a book. How much more for this complex world and marvelous universe made by that infinite Designer and Creator, the Lord Jesus Christ!

The Bible says man is created in the image and likeness of God. That is, man has a spiritual part to him, yet is fallen in sin. The *ATP rotary 'motor' bears some resemblance to the "wheels" described for the created cherubims, and for the eternal (self-existent) God Himself. No matter if all the physical components of man could be materially assembled perfectly there would still be no life in him, because there is no spiritual component. The third quote below concerns man.

> * *"And when the living creatures (cherubims) went, the wheels went by them: and when the living creatures were lifted up from the earth, the wheels were lifted up...for the spirit of the living creatures was in the wheel."* (Ezekiel 1:19-20)
>
> *"I beheld till the thrones were cast down, and the Ancient of days (God) did sit, whose garment was white as snow, and the hair of his head like the pure wool: his throne was like the fiery flame, and his wheels as burning fire."* (Daniel 7:9)
>
> *"For as the body without the spirit is dead, so faith without works is dead also."* (James 2:26)

Modern science overlooks this most important part of knowledge coming from the Word of God. Secular scientists have no interest in looking into these matters. Even with the unveiling of the human genome, showing it to be a product of design by a Supreme Being, Darwinists continue to look for loopholes in the genetic code of man, seeking to prove ape-to-man evolution.

**"Since the time of Darwin, paleoanthropologists have been obsessively trying to force the fossil record into an ape-to-man progression" – (but can't make sense of their disjointed, tangled "bush"). Taken at face value (the fossils) consist of a series of individual branching trees, suggesting each species lived side-by-side, with no common ancestor." (Rupe, C., and Sanford, J., 2017, Contested Bones, p. 333)**

Recent research on the human genome has overturned the Darwinists arguments one after another. In willful ignorance they have called large parts of the genome "junk," only to find out later that their "junk" was functional and extraordinarily complex, requiring super-intelligent design. Below is a brief summary of some of this genetic evidence from Chapter 13 in Rupe and Sanford's book, *"Contested Bones" (2017)*:

1. Life is literally programmed...the program that specifies "human being" must be incredibly advanced and incredibly specific in order to explain mankind's unique capabilities...biological information systems could never have arisen by trial and

error; ape-to-man would require a vast network of mutually dependent, massively-integrated genetic changes...never in any amount of time could this come by mutation and natural selection;

2. Truly beneficial mutations are extremely rare – can't be accurately measured...random changes will degrade useful information leading to de-evolution in the long run;
3. The waiting time problem in a hominin population – ape-to-man widely believed to take 6 million years in a population of 10,000...BUT 2 co-dependent mutations would take 84 million years; 5 mutations would exceed the age of the earth; 8 specific mutations would require 18 billion years...and only 8 nucleotides have information equivalent to "no" or "yes;"
4. Human mutation rate is 100 mutations per person per generation, and almost none of them are beneficial, but deleterious...ENCODE found that most of the human genome is functional...therefore most random change in the genome must be deleterious..."mutations work with existing information, but never add new information to the genome...If ENCODE IS RIGHT THEN EVOLUTION IS WRONG" (Evolutionary geneticist Dan Graur, U. of Houston);
5. Most bad mutations are too subtle to be selectively removed...only the worst deleterious mutations can be selected away...all the rest accumulate like the rust on a car...causing all populations to move toward extinction..."Why aren't we (humans) dead 100 X over?" (biologist's question);
6. Refuting ape-to man (A) Human/Chimp DNA similarity – 90% now...even 1% is 30 million genetic letter differences; COMMON DESIGN DOES NOT MEAN COMMON ANCESTRY;
7. Refuting ape-to man (B) Shared mutational mistakes (Junk DNA) – ENCODE shows that "junk" in our genome is actually functional and essential to life..."shared mistakes" now known to be shared functions supporting similarity by design;
8. Refuting ape-to-man (C) "Junk DNA" Beta-globin pseudogene is not a mistake but is actively transcribed, highly functional and essential to maintaining health (shared design);
9. Refuting ape-to-man (D) Vitamin C pseudogene – rat GULO gene never there to begin with as humans and apes can get Vitamin C in their natural environment from fruit and vegetables (common design, not common ancestry);
10. Refuting ape-to-man (E) Shared dispersed repeats ("selfish genes") – long DNA sequences scattered throughout the genome, like a sentence repeated many times in a book – called useless, "junk DNA." (e.g. (2004) "Alus have no known biological function." NOW (2013) new discoveries show they encode many diverse functions that are vital to life, and operate on a very high level of genomic organization...SEQUENCE SIMILARITY DOES NOT MEAN FUNCTIONAL EQUIVALENCE NOR DOES IT PROVE COMMON ANCESTRY;
11. Refuting ape-to-man (F) Chromosome 2 fusion model – 1991 claimed 'fusion' of 2 chimp chromosomes (12 & 13) to 2 similar halves of human chromosome

2 (RFS – 'reputed fusion site'), fusions generally v. deleterious and evidence of genetic entropy, reduced size of chr 2 to 2 fusing chrs., RFS NOW appears to be uniquely human DNA that is absent in ape chromosomes, entire human chr 2 has NO HOMOLOGY with the 2 chimp chromosomes, no chimp/ape "satellite" sequences flanking the RFS supposed 'fusion,' absence of large, ape-like tandem repeat between RFS and adjoining DDX11L2 'pseudogene' ("junk DNA") – NOW know that the RFS is a functional part of the DDX11L2 gene...it is NOT A FUSION SITE at all proved by Tomkins in 2017, entire RCC is not disabled but is too human and internal to a functional gene similar to RFS. NO FUSION OR GENETIC APE-TO-MAN ANCESTRY."

In the last 20 years the Darwinist's genetic 'evidence' for ape-to-man evolution has been overturned. Materially-minded men continue to resist this genetic evidence – the very strongest proof against human or any other kind of biological evolution. They have too much to lose to raise the white flag of surrender. Professor Dawkins fell back on his "self-replicating cell," but when queried where it came from he said, "No one knows." (Stein, B., 2008, Expelled – No Intelligence Allowed)

> "It is not sufficient to invoke bio-chemicals arising spontaneously. Life isn't based on bio-chemicals. You can add all the proteins, amino acids, RNA, DNA and membranes to your bio-chemical soup but they will never adhere to a coherent, correctly assembled cell – and even if they could you still wouldn't be anywhere near creating life." (Sanford, J., 2014, Evolution's Achilles' Heels)

> *"The wise men are ashamed, they are dismayed and taken: lo, they have rejected the word of the LORD; and what wisdom is in them?"* (Jeremiah 8:9)

Every created "kind" (i.e., genus/genera) was capable of a high degree of variation within boundaries controlled by the coded information in that specific organism's genome. Variations came through adaptation to a multitude of changing conditions in the ecosystem. Natural selection and variation of each "kind" were constrained within these God-designed limits. That is why it would be possible to put all the human diversity on earth into a single human couple. That is why it is possible to obtain 1,500 varieties of Hawthorne plants by natural variation, but never see one change into a rose; and 500 varieties of mosquito, but none morphing into a housefly. That is why man can breed many kinds of dogs, cats and horses; but never cross the fixed boundaries between them. That is why there are 15,000 different fossil trilobites, but they are all trilobites. These created kinds are on display today if you walk in the woods, take a tour through an aquarium, a zoo, or a fossil collection; or examine fossil sequences in the rock record as the writer has seen in the field and in his subsurface thesis studies. Darwin's tree of life, and its multitudinous 'missing links' is nowhere to be seen anywhere, not now in 2021, nor in 1859 when he wrote *On the Origin of Species*. Biological life is likened to a grove or an orchard of created kinds (genera), not evolution from a single, self-replicating cell that came to live by chance. Evolutionists grasp frantically for "the missing link" but are blinded to the reality of the created kinds all around them today in the real world. As a geologist I find this really sad – even tragic. Man's heart is deeply corrupted by sin and that is why secular science and academia are in their present deplorable condition.

The "Cambrian Explosion" left Darwin in a '541 million year' quandary. An intact marine ecosystem with most major phyla suddenly appears in the rock record with no sign of evolution back to a few original, or even singular, progenitor(s) anywhere in the rock record. None has ever been found. And the same phyla remain well-defined to the present day, notwithstanding many extinctions. The Middle Cambrian Burgess Shale of Western Canada formed in an oxygen-starved (anerobic) environment where up to 115,000 species have been preserved. An amazing array of soft-and-hard bodied, complex organisms that defy Darwin's theory of evolution, and his statement that "no organism wholly soft can be preserved," (*On the Origin of Species*, p. 124) are preserved in these black shales. They include sponges, soft-bodied arthropods, and those with hard exoskeletons, the first chorelates, worms and trilobites; and a strange, spiked creature that has been named, *wiwaxia*.

He felt certain that some of the multitudes of paleontological 'missing links' would eventually be found in the future in the geological rock record. They haven't materialized in the 160$^{+}$ years since his book was written despite millions and millions more fossils being collected and categorized worldwide. They will never be found, because they don't exist. The "Orchard of Creation" (Evolution's Achilles' Heels, 2014) described in Genesis Chapter 1 fits the data, not Darwin's one or two progenitors from some dark, immemorial past conjured up by his fantastic imagination. God created many "kinds;" of animals, plants and marine organisms, each with its specialized genome capable of producing many varieties or species **(Figure 15)**. Each tree could be likened to a single genus. There were enough living creatures to warrant building an ark 450 feet in length, 45 feet high and 75 feet wide. The same phylum-level organisms seen in the sudden burst of life in the Lower Cambrian are still seen today in marine waters, supposedly over 500 million years later. A look at the world around us will show the same diversity of living organisms in the air, water and on the land that were there when God spoke them into existence in Genesis Chapter 1.

**Figure 15**

Created "kinds" (genera) of Genesis Chapter 1 are likened to a grove or an orchard with each original kind's DNA genetically controlling its species variability.

Charles Darwin (1809-1882), the self-described ***naturalist**, did not believe in the created "kinds" (genera) mentioned in Genesis Chapter 1. With his mass of descriptive facts he jumps from one detail of morphology to another; from birds to insects, from plants to animals of all kinds - around and around and around; and then with one vast sweep of his imagination brings it all together into some "early progenitor" backed up by Charles Lyell's "eons and vast periods of time," from which all life occurring in nature supposedly evolved. His materialistic reasoning trumps a supernatural God being the Creator. His accumulation of facts and analogies is simply overwhelming for most people to read. They get lost in the details as he tries to persuade them that "secondary factors" and natural selection explain the life we see on earth today, and not God or intelligent design. He often mentions, "I can see no explanation...for independent creation...of species...is erroneous." "Secondary causes" in the natural, material environment with the struggle and survival of the fittest defining which species evolved and which became extinct. Darwin frequently refers with admiration of his friend, "Sir Charles Lyell," the nineteenth century geologist and his long geological ages with "the present is the key to the past" concept. Tragically, this is where *"science falsely so-called,"* (1 Timothy 6:20) still remains entrenched and mired today.

*__naturalist:__ One who has made a special study of natural objects, as plants, minerals, and, especially animals. One who believes that all phenomena are traceable to natural (produced by nature) causes. (The Winston Dictionary, 1946)

Darwin wrote that the "Creator" breathed life into his few primordial archetype(s), at the end of *On the Origin of Species* (first ed.), but this creator remains impersonal and anonymous. Professor Owen, addressing the British Association in 1858, said, "by the word 'creation' the zoologist means 'a process he knows not what."' (Appendix - An Historical Sketch on the Progress of Opinion *On the Origin of Species*, p. 212). This definition fits Darwin's use of the term, Creator, in its context in his book; a nebulous entity. In fact, Darwin said just that -

> "In a letter to Hooker dated March 1863, Darwin discussed this incident, noting that, 'It will be sometime before we see slime, snot, or protoplasm generating a new animal. But I have long regretted that I truckled to public opinion & used the Pentateuchal term of creation, by which I really meant 'appeared' by some wholly unknown process'...Darwin insisted his theory of evolution must be godless to be scientific...at his core Darwin was in fact an atheist even though he denied this, no doubt in deference to his devout wife and his scientific friends who were believers." (Bergman, J., 2011, The Dark Side of Charles Darwin, pp. 67-68, 71-72)

The concept of evolution is based upon the assumption of long periods of time measured in the millions and billions of years. It is the guiding principle for 'dating' the fossils and geological processes we see in the world around us. It is the core paradigm in the ape-to-man evolutionary idea. It drives people's thinking; it boxes them in so they can't interpret scientific data at face value. Evolution teaches the extinction of species which could not compete for survival, but it cannot tell us about the "arrival of the fittest." Professor Dawkins with his 2 degrees in Zoology made that very clear in his interview with Ben Stein (pp. 105-107).

If evolution is true there is no rational basis for morality. Marxist movements advocate the tearing down and destroying of traditional Judeo-Christian culture and replacing it with a supposedly 'superior' socialist-communist utopia like George Orwell's "1984." They don't care who or what they liquidate or destroy to get there. To the political left, it is survival of the fittest ideology, meaning only Darwinian social evolution. In their minds, they are the only ones enlightened and qualified enough to pilot the ship of government and society to a 'better' future. Chinese Xi Jinping said as much in a recent article in The Epoch Times. Chinese Communism embraced Darwinism as soon as it took control of China in 1949. The CCP is looking at international relations in a social Darwinian context, meaning the survival of the fittest society and nation - namely "socialism with Chinese characteristics."

"China's leader Xi Jinping claims that today's world is characterized by a "chaos" not seen in 100 years...created by the COVID-19 pandemic, and that China has curbed the outbreak successfully..."it shows immediately which country's leadership and political system is good," he said...and the timing and circumstances all favour China and can help the Chinese Communist Party (CCP) to reach its goal of world domination." (Hao, N., May 13, 2021, Xi Jinping Talks Chaos: Pandemic Provides Favourable Conditions for CCP Domination, The Epoch Times)

**"Marx and Engel's acceptance of evolutionary theory made it the basis of all later Communist ideology. Marxism is closely linked to Darwinism (i.e., "struggle"). Lenin was an ardent evolutionist and so was Stalin. Chinese Communists eagerly grasped evolutionary theory in 1950 as a basic foundation of their ideology." (Ferrell, V., 2001, The Evolution Handbook, pp. 810, 819-21)**

Darwinian philosophy accepts that human lives are just a bag of chemicals; they don't matter, because there is no creation, no purpose beyond the material world here and now. Karl Marx commended Darwin on his *"On the Origin of Species"* (1859) claiming that it gave him support for his dialectical materialism, that is, socialism-communism. Hitler wrote *Mein Kampf* (My Struggle), publicly embracing Darwinian evolution and using it to promote the destruction of his 'lower races' (Jews, Slavs, Gypsies, the infirm and the handicapped) and the exaltation of his "superior" Aryan race. Mao Zedong claimed he was a disciple of Marx, and had no problem liquidating millions. He taught and mentored Pol Pot who did the same. China's Xi Jinping patterns himself after Mao. Who knows what he or one of his successors has planned for the future? Darwin himself wrote racially incendiary evolutionary statements that established the basis for this kind of thinking. As a boy and young man he had an inordinate lust to kill animals, not for food only, but for the pure excitement and desire to kill. It extended into his lab work on animals in later years as well.

"The more civilized so-called Caucasian races have beaten the Turkish hollow in the struggle for existence. Looking to the world at no distant date, what an endless number of the lower races will have been eliminated by the higher civilized races throughout the world." (Ferrell, V., 2001, The Evolution Handbook, p. 822 – quoting Charles Darwin, Life and Letters, p. 318)

"Darwin was psychologically a very troubled man for most of his life. He evidently suffered from an inordinate sadistic desire to kill animals for much of his life, especially when he was a young man in the prime of life...Darwin's obsession went well beyond this (liking hunting). He loved to kill and, apparently, loved to see animals suffer." (Bergman, J., 2011, The Dark Side of Charles Darwin, pp. 133-134)

It seems that the inordinate desire to kill has followed Darwinian ideology, patterning itself after the manner of the man who wanted to "murder God," and destroy faith in Biblical Christianity. Darwin certainly succeeded in leading mankind into a spree of bloodshed and killing greater than ever before in the history of humanity. The killing continues to the present day (including abortion and euthanasia), promising to become even worse in the future as mankind sheds all belief in the God of Creation and Redemption.

Darwin's theory of evolution is at the heart of the conflict in society in the Western nations today. It is leftist; it is racist. It controls the narrative in science, philosophy, education, the judiciary, social relationships and individual morality. Most of the population has been taught evolution, or its camouflaged precepts, in various courses in their secondary school and college education classes, helping to bring Western society to its present morally degenerate condition. We are living on the brink of a new Dark Age. Dr. John Sanford, a Cornell University adjunct professor and expert in genetic entropy, comments on his personal experience as a Christian questioning Darwin's teachings at the college level. In "Evolution's Achilles' Heels," 2014, he says,

> "What I find is that most evolutionists have never critically examined their own position. It is such a sacred cow in their minds it is unthinkable to start examining their own weaknesses. **It is an amazing stronghold**. You know if you want to consider yourself pure intellectually you must be a Darwinist; it's that simple. It's like a fee you pay for getting into the club. And so this is a very, very, strong motivator, and there is a flip side to that, which is, if you don't hold it, you will be ridiculed, and will be treated as if you are really stupid and ignorant, and so the fear of ridicule is just palpable on campuses. Many, many scientists actually realize that there are major problems with Darwinian Theory but they are silent because they know if they speak their doubts they will get in trouble. They won't get grants; they won't get funding; they won't be politically correct; they won't have friends; all the stuff that makes for academic success goes away if you question Darwin."
>
> "There's another reason why evolutionists will hold onto their belief system when all the fatal flaws are revealed; and, that is, because if evolution isn't true it strongly points them in a different direction."
>
> *"Because that which may be known of God is manifest in them; for God hath shewed it unto them. For the invisible things of him from the creation of the world are clearly seen, being understood by the things that are made, even his eternal power and Godhead; so that they are without excuse;"* (Romans 1:19-20)
>
> "Because if the universe and life didn't self-create; if it didn't happen spontaneously, then there has to be a Creator, and the Creator is not likely to be some little green man from another galaxy. The Creator is going to be Almighty God."
>
> "Salvation doesn't result from intellectual activity; it doesn't come through figuring out God or theology. **It is a spiritual transaction**."
>
> *"That if thou shalt confess with thy mouth the Lord Jesus, and shalt believe in thine heart that God hath raised him from the dead, thou shalt be saved."* (Romans 10:9)

"So, for me, when I understood that God made a perfect creation: *"In the beginning God created the heaven and the earth."* (Genesis 1:1); there was a literal fall; and now God is restoring us by the sacrifice of His Son, it really transformed my faith. For, although I was a Christian for 10 years, I was an incredibly weak Christian; and so every aspect of my life was transformed by more fully submitting to God by believing His Word."

*"For thus saith the LORD that created the heavens; God himself that formed the earth and made it; he hath established it, he created it not in vain, he formed it to be inhabited: I am the LORD; and there is none else."* (Isaiah 45:18)

**Ben Stein confronted one of Darwinian evolution's modern architects, Oxford Professor Richard Dawkins, in an interview in the DVD *"Expelled – No Intelligence Allowed,"* 2008. Portions of this interview show the evolutionary mindset that has a stranglehold over academia today. Dr. Dawkins published his book, "*The God Delusion,*" in October, 2006. It became a million seller. In an earlier book, he wrote:**

**"that instead of 'examining the evidence for and against rival theories [of the origins of life], I shall adapt a more armchair approach. My argument will be that Darwinism is the only known theory that is in principle *capable* of explaining [the origins of life]...even if there were no actual evidence in favor of the Darwinian theory...we should still be justified in preferring it over all rival theories."' (Bergman, J., 2011, The Dark Side of Charles Darwin, p. 55)**

**B.S. Professor Dawkins seemed so certain God didn't exist, I wondered if he would be willing to put a number on it.**

**R.D. It's hard to put a number on it, but I'd guess it would be 99%**

**B.S. Why 99%, and not 97%?**

**R.D. You asked me to put a number on it; and I'm not comfortable putting a number on it. I just think it is very unlikely.**

**B.S. But you couldn't put a number on it. So then, it could be 49%. What about 49%?**

**R.D. It's unlikely; but it's quite far from 50%**

**B.S. How do you know?**

**R.D. I don't know but it's just very unlikely. I put an argument in the book.**

B.S. Well then; who did create the heavens and the earth?

R.D. Why do you use the word 'Who?' You immediately beg the question by using the word 'Who.'

B.S. Well then, how did it get created?

R.D. Well then, by a very slow process.

B.S. Well, how did it start?

R.D. We don't know how it started, but we know the kind of events it must have been – the sort of events that must have happened for the origin of life. It was the start of the first self-replicating molecule.

B.S. And how did that happen?

R.D. I've told you; I don't know.

B.S. So, you have no idea how it started?

R.D. No – nor has anyone else.

B.S. What do you think of the possibility that intelligent design might turn out to be the answer to some issues in genetics or in the doctrine of evolution?

R.D. It could come about in the following way. It could be that in some earlier time somewhere in the universe, a civilization evolved by some kind of Darwinian means to a very, very high level of technology and designed a form of life that was perhaps seeded onto this planet (i.e., *directed panspermia*). That is a possibility, an intriguing possibility, and I suppose it's possible you might find evidence of that if you look at the detailed cells in biochemistry or molecular biology; a signature of some sort of designer.

B.S. Wait a second! Richard Dawkins thought intelligent design might be a legitimate pursuit, and that designer could well be a higher intelligence from elsewhere in the universe.

R.D. And that intelligence itself would have had to have come about by some explicable or ultimately explicable process. It couldn't have just jumped into existence spontaneously – that's the point.

B.S. So, Professor Dawkins is not against intelligent design, just certain types of designer – such as God.

B.S. So, the Hebrew God, the God of the Old Testament. He doesn't exist in your view?

R.D. Certainly not! That would be a very unpleasant prospect.

**B.S. What about the Holy Trinity of the New Testament?**

**R.D. Nothing like that.**

**B.S. Do you believe in any of the Hindu gods?**

**R.D. How can you ask such a question? How could I? Why would I, if I don't believe in any others?**

**B.S. Or the Moslem gods?**

**R.D. No. Why do you even need to ask?**

**B.S. I just wanted to be sure. So, you don't believe in any God, anywhere?**

**R.D. Any God anywhere would be completely incompatible with anything that I've said.**

**B.S. What if after you died you ran into God, and He said, "What have you been doing Richard? I've been trying to be nice to you. I've given you a multi-million dollar paycheque, over and over again, from your book – and look what you did."**

**R.D. Bertrand Russell had this point put to him, and he said, "Sir, why did you take such pains to hide yourself?"**

**God never tried to hide Himself. He gave us a Book, the Bible. In it, He reveals Himself as the Creator (Isaiah 45:18). His creation testifies of His eternal power and Godhead (Romans 1:19-20). It is man that tries to hide from God; and that is exactly what the proponents of evolution are doing. Professor Dawkins said it would be a very unpleasant prospect if the Hebrew God existed. In his earlier book he said he wasn't willing even to consider that prospect. Why? Because he would have to face Him in judgment for his sin. Dawkins' reliance upon intelligent design from another civilization elsewhere in the universe seeding life on earth is called *directed panspermia*. Since he could not explain how life first began he looked outside the earth for it in a highly intelligent and technical civilization – but absolutely NOT to the God of the Bible. Where did his imagined super-civilization come from? He is trapped by circular reasoning that ends up at God. Dr. Jonathan Sarfati said the following about the evolutionist's escape to fantasy in *directed panspermia*, a wonderland somewhere in outer space:**

"Evolutionists who resort to *directed panspermia* are in fact tacitly conceding that life was intelligently designed. The only difference is their designer is an alien and not the God of the Bible. And of course, this is most convenient for them because the God of the Bible has certain moral requirements while aliens don't. So, they can have all the benefits of a designer without the moral obligations to Him. Now there are some moral obligations here (e.g. Exodus 20:13 – re: murder). If the Creator made us, He owns us, and has a right to set rules for us. But, if things make themselves, then there is no right or wrong, we're just bags of re-arranged pond scum, so what is murder? It is just one bag of chemicals impacting another bag of chemicals. Science can't tell you that murder is right or wrong. It can tell you this action will kill something, but it won't tell you it's right or wrong." (Evolution's Achilles' Heels, 2014)

"In spite of the discoveries of modern science that have shown the Evolutionary Theory to be a figment of an ungodly imagination, a shoddy fraud inspired of the devil himself, the professors of our Universities are still assiduously seeking to support the Theory, and trying to indoctrinate all new students (poor unsuspecting souls) with its teachings." (The Prophetic Voice, July, 1947, Evolution Cross-examined)

Professor Dawkins, a militant atheist, went on after this interview to write more books attacking God and Biblical Christianity. In *The Dark Side of Charles Darwin: A Critical Analysis of an Icon of Science*, 2011, Jerry Bergman quotes this famous atheist as he describes the Darwinian concept of a purposeless universe, where purposeless life spontaneously arose from non-life. Dr. Dawkins' "self-replicating cell" (in the interview above) is addressed in the second quote below. It comes from a reliance upon Darwinian teaching. Thinking like this led to Darwin's eugenics described in Bergman's book (Chapter 12) and ultimately to its application in real life in Hitler's Third Reich as outlined in "Expelled: No Intelligence Allowed," by Ben Stein, 2008. Society is going in that direction again.

"Humans have always wondered about the meaning of life." The fact is "life has no higher purpose [other] than to perpetuate the survival of the DNA." "Some people are going to get hurt, other people are going to get lucky, and you won't find any rhyme or reason in it, nor any justice. The universe we observe has precisely the properties we should expect if there is, at bottom, no design, no purpose, no evil and no good, nothing but

**blind, pitiless indifference." (Dawkins quoted in The Dark Side of Charles Darwin, pp. 76 & 80)**

**(Darwin's) "Pangenesis is actually a Lamarckian idea because it teaches that factors, such as exercise or learning, can cause changes in body cells that are passed on to one's progeny – 'the theory of transmission of acquired characteristics.' The transfer of worldly acquisitions from the environment to offspring was a sort of spontaneous generation of life from non-life, and this was evolution. Darwin never thought that evolution was anything else, and he would have disapproved the Theory of Evolution propounded in his name in the twentieth century." (Bergman, J., 2011, The Dark Side of Charles Darwin, pp. 194-195)**

**If a man is willing to be taught, the best teacher is God, and the best 'assistant' teachers are His creation, including His creatures. The Book of Job declares plainly this truth as follows:**

***"But ask now the beasts, and they shall teach thee; and the fowls of the air, and they shall tell thee: Or speak to the earth, and it shall teach thee: and the fishes of the sea shall declare unto thee. Who knoweth not in all these things that the hand of the LORD hath wrought this?*** **(Job 12:7-10)**

***"All flesh is not the same flesh: but there is on kind of flesh of men, another flesh of beasts, another of fishes, and another of birds."*** **(I Corinthians 15:39)**

**It would be impossible for these different kinds of flesh to evolve. They are distinct and were created that way in the beginning. We have learned about one beast, "behemoth," in Chapter 6. Speaking to Job out of the whirlwind, God expressly stated he made that animal with its specific adaptations – and reserved the right to destroy it (i.e. extinction). Concerning the fowls, God adapted the majestic eagle to soar on the air currents with minimal effort of flight. Recent airliners adopt this specific upturn at the wing tip that the eagles have. It took a long time for the airlines to 'get it.'**

"The eagle has six slotted feathers at the tip of each wing which curve upward in gliding flight. Our wind tunnel measurements indicated that these upward-curved slotted-tip feathers reduce the size of the vortex emanating from each wing tip. This in turn reduces the drag on the wings, thus allowing the eagle to soar large distances in air currents without the need of beating its wings." (Blick, E., 1986, Creation and Noah's Ark, p. 14)

*"But they that wait upon the LORD shall renew their strength; they shall mount up with wings as eagles; they shall run, and not be weary; and they shall walk, and not faint."* (Isaiah 40:31)

The fish has been designed specifically for the element in which it lives.

"The shape of the fish is specifically designed to meet the pressure problem of underwater life. We make our ships, and particularly our submersibles, exactly after this pattern, and we call ourselves intelligent because we do this. The floating and locomotor apparatus of the fish is perfect for its need. Its scales form a perfect protection for its body, being composed of the same material as horse's hooves. The edge of each scale forms an oil-skin waterproof jacket, so that the fish, living in water, actually does NOT GET WET! Its gills separate air from the water in a marvelous manner. The eyes of the fish are able to see in every direction, to watch for its enemies. They are shaped to meet the water pressure, and their design is copied in our diving suits and helmets. Fish that feed on very small things have eyes that magnify in exact ratio to the minuteness of their food. And the Malaysian fish even have bi-focal lenses; the lower half magnifies the tiny food upon which it lives, while the upper half is long-sighted, so that it can watch out for the gulls that prey upon it!" (The Prophetic Voice, April, 1944, The Mystery of the Swimming Fish)

*"His scales are his pride, shut up together as with a close seal. One is so near to another, that no air can come between them. They are joined one to another, they stick together, that they cannot be sundered."* (Job 41:15-17)

Even the earth 'speaks' through God's hand that shaped it; the natural processes being the instruments He used to do His work. We have seen this in Chapters 2 through 8, the last referring to the migration of mankind over the earth. An eminent archeologist, Professor J. O. Kinnaman commented –

"Of all the hundreds of thousands of artifacts which have been found bearing DIRECTLY upon the Bible, not one has ever been found that denies, contradicts, obscures or belittles one word, phrase, clause or sentence of either the Old or New Testaments; but they invariably verify, confirm, illuminate, illustrate and fill in the historical gaps." (The Prophetic Voice, October, 1944, The Earth Speaks! Archeologists Amazing Discoveries – No. 1)

"Life as we know it here on earth is insupportable anywhere else…The axis of the earth is tilted at an angle of 23.5° to the plane of the earth's orbit and thus we have the four seasons of the year. If the axis of the earth were in a vertical position we would have no seasons at all. There could be no summer or winter, or freezing or thawing. Then ice would begin to accumulate at the poles in increasing masses until the seas of the earth were dried up, or until they became too salty to support marine life, like the Dead Sea. Then rainfall would practically disappear, and the earth would become a desert. Human life, and all other life, depends on that exact angle of inclination which brings us our seasons. Again, if the earth's axis was in a horizontal position, one half of the earth would lie in continual, frozen night, and the other half would receive all the heat of the sun, remaining in perpetual day. Would not this result in an earth half burning desert, and half glacial wilderness? And if the earth did not turn on its axis at just the right speed it would disrupt the cycle of life and the balance of the law of gravity. Who set the speed of the earth around the sun, so that its centrifugal force, as it swings on its elliptical orbit, exactly balances the sun's attraction, so that it neither falls toward the sun, nor flies off into outer space? If the earth went infinitesimally slower, it would soon burn up and slowly fall into the sun. If it went a fraction faster, it would gradually swing out farther and farther into frozen space, and all life would perish. Five percent more or less heat would ruin the world. The sun, at its present power and distance is just right for life on this earth. If our moon were larger the ocean tides would flood our harbors and lowlands. If it were smaller the tides would not be enough to cleanse the smallest harbors, and terrible pollution would soon poison our coasts." (The Prophetic Voice, November, 1946, Evolution Cross-examined!)

*"He stretcheth out the north over the empty place, and hangeth the earth upon nothing…By his spirit he hath garnished the heavens."* (Job 26:7, 13)

Man has been given every faculty to know the truth, but sadly, he has deliberately chosen to believe a lie – and that lie is Darwinian evolution. Theistic evolution is equally false. At the heart of any kind of 'evolution is a heart of unbelief – in God's Word. Faith is at issue here. God has created man in His own likeness and image with the intellectual capacity to study and know His Word, the Bible. Man deliberately chooses not to do that by an act of his own free will. Yet, man is accountable to his Creator. Professor Dawkins thought that would be a very unpleasant prospect; and he was right. There is a heaven to gain and a hell to shun.

*"And God said, Let us make man in our image, after our likeness: and let them have dominion over the fish of the sea, and over the fowl of the air, and over the cattle, and over all the earth, and over every creeping thing that creepeth upon the earth. So God created man in his own image, in the image of God created he him; male and female created he them."* (Genesis 1:26-27)

"*Homo sapiens* (man) appears as distinctive and unprecedented…there is certainly no evidence to support the notion we gradually became who we inherently are over an extended period, in either the physical or intellectual sense." (Curator of the American Museum of Natural History, 2012, (in Rupe et al, 2017, Contested Bones, p. 26)

"Only humans can do science, sequence their own genome, reason, engineer cities, visit the moon, write books/programs/poetry/music, or show agape love. Biblically, only man is a moral being with a soul, capable of communion with God. In all these respects we are incredibly unique." (Ibid, p. 347)

"There are many physical peculiarities found in man which completely distinguish him from the lower animals, and render the Theory of Evolution quite untenable." (The Prophetic Voice, June, 1943, It's a Fact)

1. Man is without any protective covering, such as the animals enjoy. This is no advantage developed by evolution. It calls into play the highly developed intelligence of man, in the construction of tools for the making of necessary garments.
2. Man possesses a brain weighing more than twice as much as that of a gorilla. Man must have such a brain to give him the intelligence he needs. It would only be an encumbrance to an unintelligent animal.
3. The whole structure of the human body is distinct from all other forms. The ball and socket joints in the hip bones and the adjustment of all the vertebrae of the back and neck give man his erect posture. No animal has these features in the slightest degree, and therefore can never walk naturally erect. Man is a biped, never a quadraped.
4. Man's intellectual capacity belongs to an entirely different order than that of animals. Romanes, after collecting the manifestations of intelligent reasoning from every known species of animal, found that they equaled IN TOTAL the intelligence of a child only 15 months old.
5. Man is a tool-making and tool-using creature. Animals are not.
6. Man is a fire-using creature. No animals ever make or use fire.
7. Man is a speaking and writing creature. Try to train the most cultivated monkey to translate and understand some ancient inscription unearthed from the ruins of a deserted city!
8. Man is a religious creature, with a consciousness of the existence of a Supreme Being. The lowest man worships something. The animal in its highest development never does.

Such evidence cannot be waved aside. It marks man as a special creation from the hand of an Omnipotent and Omniscient God!"

***"For it is written, As I live, saith the Lord, every knee shall bow to me, and every tongue shall confess to God. So then every one of us shall give account of himself to God."* (Romans 14:11-12)**

# CONCLUSIONS

The Bible says that the earth is young. The genealogies of the patriarchs before and after the Flood give an age of about 6000 years. Noah's Flood (2348 B.C.) and the time span of the "days of Peleg" (2250 – 2000 B.C.) provide two major earth upheavals that are documented in the Bible and that can be correlated with scientific data indicating a young earth. The global sea level chart shows two such "megacycles" which involved rapid deposition of thick sedimentary deposits worldwide accompanied by catastrophic geological processes all of which showed rapid entropy between the Flood year and the end of the "days of Peleg," a period encompassing only about 350 to 400 years. It was at this time that most of the sedimentary rock record was deposited and the mountains we see today formed.

1. The Book of Job is the oldest in the Bible with patriarchs that had lived during the "days of Peleg:" its scientific pronouncements are geologically valid, as are the rest of the Bible's.
2. Patriarchs gave eye witness accounts of rapid seafloor spreading and continental drift: both beginning during Noah's Flood and concluding at about the end of the "days of Peleg."
3. Patriarchs gave witness of mountain building during their lifetimes: tight folding without fracturing of brittle rocks indicates young ages for mountain ranges; carbon-14 within folded coals shows the mountains formed during Noah's Flood and the "days of Peleg."
4. Patriarchs gave witness of rapid uplift and subsidence in which thick sediments accumulated in basins and along continental margins: carbon-14 and dinosaur bones with preserved soft tissues within these rocks indicates a young earth age for sedimentary formations deposited since Noah's Flood, and even for diamonds in rocks in the Early Precambrian crust below Noah's Flood deposits.
5. Patriarchs lived at the same time as dinosaurs: preserved soft tissues, bone cells and DNA in cells corroborate the young earth age of dinosaur bones and their enclosing sedimentary rocks.
6. Man migrated to the New World before the earth was divided during Peleg's days: genetic tracing and archeology indicates migration patterns; man's migration from Babel fits the geological record correlating to the earlier migration of dinosaurs to the 'New World.'
7. Catastrophic earth processes during Noah's Flood and the "days of Peleg" provide a mechanism for glaciation within a young earth age.
8. The identification of soft tissue, including DNA and bone cells, in dinosaur bones supposedly 80 million years of age or older is unfeasible. The fossils formed during the Post-Flood period only a matter of 4000 to 4500 years ago. The presence of unstable carbon-14 in coals throughout the geologic record indicate a young earth the same as the soft tissue evidence.

9. Something is drastically wrong with the ages given by radiometric dating, including the carbon-14 method. They are not reliable because their underlying assumptions cannot be proven and are, therefore, wrong and untrustworthy.
10. Biblical chronology and the scientific evidence indicate that the earth is only about 6000 years old to the present time.

***"The Book of Job and Biblical Chronology"*** mainly concerns the Post-Flood period where the history of earth processes and stratigraphic record are defined in relation to the "days of Peleg," and shown within the contents in the preceding chapters. We find that many profound geological phenomena are described in accurate detail and reveal eyewitness characteristics. We read of the physical splitting apart of the earth, the dividing of the seas, mountains being overturned by the roots, mighty rivers drying up, ice breaking forth and giant animals that are representative of the dinosaurs. None of these descriptions contradict other Scriptures; they are in perfect harmony creating a complete picture of earth history in a human historical context.

Geological uniformitarianism is a false teaching and must be declared so! The present is ***not*** the key to the past with respect to the rates of earth processes. It has helped lead nearly the entire human race away from the eternal God and His Word. The earth in its natural state, and all its processes is wearing out; it is degrading and deteriorating. God's Word says so, corroborating the Second Law of Thermodynamics (The Law of Entropy) discovered by William Thompson (Lord Kelvin) and Nicholas Carnot in the mid-nineteenth century. Man's fall and the entry of sin into the world brought about a supernatural act of God in judgment – the Flood – initiating entropy and the decay process in creation. All geological processes moved toward entropy after the fountains of the great deep were broken up during the beginning of Noah's Flood. Seafloor spreading and continental drift accompanied the earth's expansion, mountain building and deposition of sediments, volcanism, glaciation, extinction of species and the earth's magnetic field all decayed rapidly, even exponentially, to near static by the close of the days of Peleg. Near the end of Reu's and Serug's lives (2000 – 1950 B.C.) the earth had begun to stabilize. Human lifespan declined from more than 900 years before the Flood to 70 to 80 years at the time of Moses in 1500 B.C. (Psalm 90:10). This rapid unwinding of the human and geological 'clocks' took about 350 to 400 years **(Figure 16, below)**. Declining human life span followed this path of entropy in about the same time frame as the natural processes to the present day in 2021 A.D. Only the continued supernatural hand of God has held human life expectancy at 70 to 80 years for over 3500 years. Why? Because God is giving mankind a window of opportunity to repent of sin and be saved (2 Peter 3:7-9, John 3:16).

Man cannot conceive in his wildest imagination the power of God and what God can do. A statement on this fact is given in the Bible, which when carefully considered, that provides a glimpse from eternity into time, and can be used in the Biblical model for earth history.

*"But, beloved, be not ignorant of this one thing, that one day is with the Lord as a thousand years, and a thousand years as one day."* (2 Peter 3:8)

This verse of Scripture shows that *"one day with the Lord is as 1,000 years"* (365,000 days), *"and a thousand years* (365,000 days) *as one day."* The ratio for 1 day/1,000 years is (1:365,000). Now, considering the time between the Flood and the beginning of Peleg's days - about 100 years - the same ratio would yield 36,500,000 years. This means that God can do in 100 years what man thinks would many millions of years. Only God doesn't need millions of years to do it. Secular 'geologic time' is a trap which man has fallen into by his human reasoning process and rejection of the Word of God. This kind of thinking is what motivated Lyell and Darwin to conceive of vast periods of time for the earth and evolution. They neglected to consider that an eternal, omnipotent God is not constrained by time or entropy. He is in complete control of all of the natural world and its laws. The Bible teaches that the fall of man and SIN brought about the decay process in nature and the human race. One day God will burn up the present heavens and earth and make a new heavens and earth in which there will be no entropy because there will be NO SIN. (2 Peter 3:12-13)

Entropy (The Second Law of Thermodynamics) is why we cannot use current rates of geological processes to dictate a vast age for the earth. It refutes the Darwinian theory of evolution and the progress of man. The radioactive decay series would also be affected by entropy because the natural world is "rusting out." The assumption of constant decay rates within a closed rock system would not be realistic in such a dynamic earth as existed between Noah's Flood and the end of Peleg's days. **Figures 1 and 16** can be viewed in concert. Only the Bible gives the ultimate answer to origins, both human and geological.

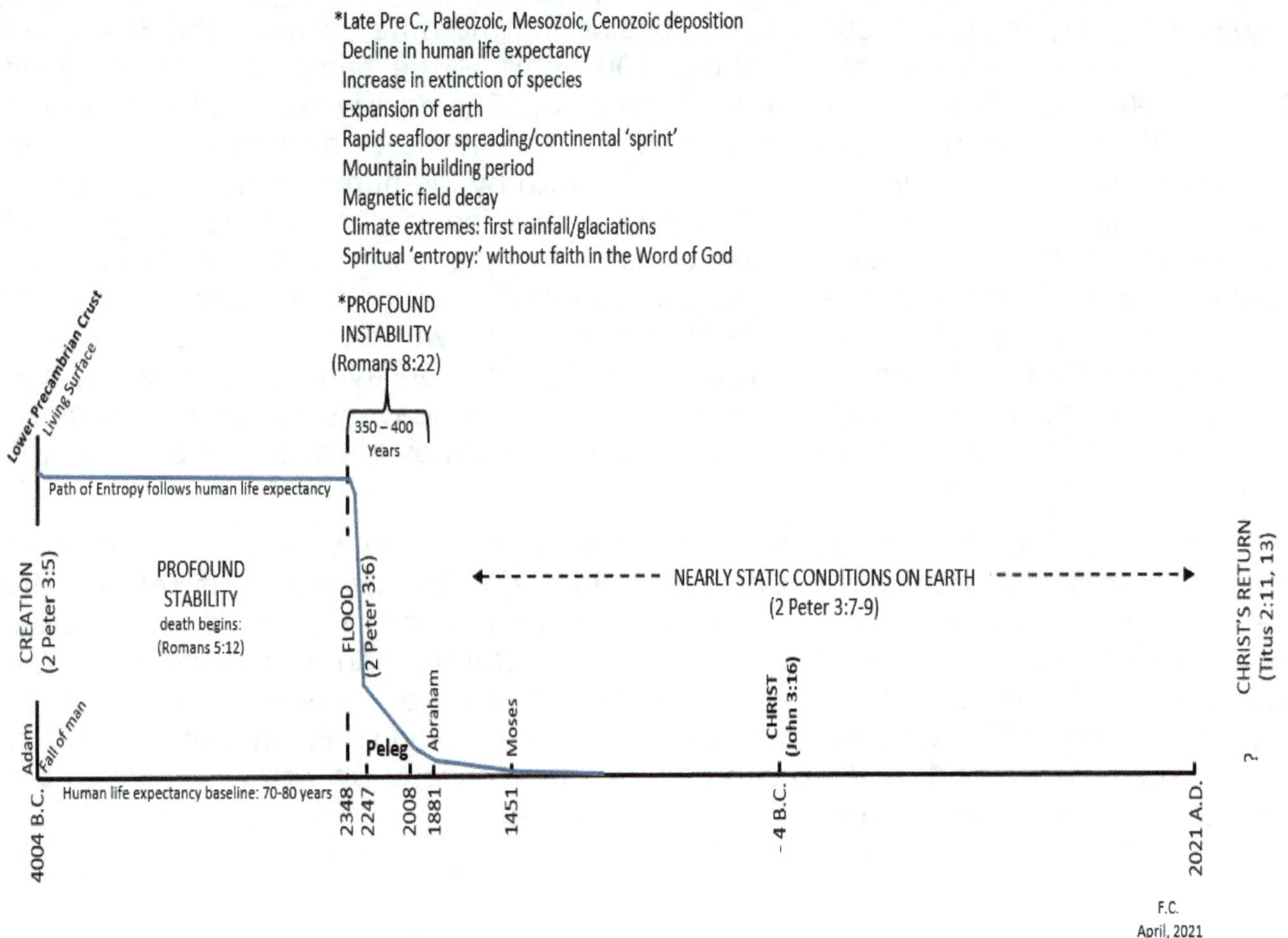


**Figure 16**

Model for earth history based upon Biblical chronology and the law of entropy

> *"Of old hast thou laid the foundation of the earth: and the heavens are the work of thy hands. They shall perish, but thou shalt endure: yea, all of them shall wax old like a garment; as a vesture shalt thou change them, and they shall be changed: But thou art the same, and thy years shall have no end."* (Psalm 102:25-27)

Scientist – don't fear reading the Bible. It will not threaten your expertise or cause you to abdicate responsible science. A person can believe the Bible and make valuable contributions to science or any other field. Honoring God and His Word will bring blessings both to academics and society. Many great scientists believed the Bible, Isaac Newton being one example. Newton wrote in his second edition of the "Principles of Mathematics," the following:

"This most beautiful system of the sun, planets, and comets could only proceed from the counsel and dominion of an intelligent and powerful being...As a blind man has no idea of colors, so we have no idea of the manner by which the all-wise God perceives and understands all things." (from The Epoch Times, 2004, "Nine Commentaries on the Communist Party," On How the Communist Party is an Anti-Universe Force – Part 4, p.9,)

We can all be thankful for research and development in modern physics, chemistry, biology and geology because they have brought many material benefits to our civilization The need today is not to reject true science but the evolutionary and uniformitarian paradigm, narrative or worldview from which they are viewed and skewed. Darwinism is an impediment to understanding ultimate origins and the processes that have shaped our earth and lives. It is retrograde 'learning.' If there is no purpose in life, then why progress? It would be good if scientists would reject this theory and its offshoots (e.g., Theistic evolution) and start believing Genesis 1:1.

*"In the beginning God created the heaven and the earth."*

The Bible is considered irrelevant to any serious scientific discussion today. Yet the previous sections illustrate a sound Biblical chronology for the Cenozoic and Mesozoic portions of the 'geologic record.' It is a serious mistake to ignore this kind of evidence because it is the key to unlocking many enigmas in science. Dr. Edward Blick, quoted below, was Professor of Aerospace, Mechanical and Nuclear Engineering at the University of Oklahoma.

"Can a man be both a scientist and a Christian? (Yes!) There is a great deal of evidence proving that there is a definite correlation between the Bible and science. Why do some scientists believe in God and yet others reject Him. We have a capacity for doubt built within us, as well as a capacity for faith, and the will of man is the determining factor. Why does one scientist, in possession of the same facts as another, believe and accept Jesus Christ and the teachings of the Bible, and the other reject Him? Since both are scientists, it couldn't be the facts of science that keep one from believing. No, it is simply that he exercises his will to doubt rather than to believe. **Faith and doubt are determined by the will, not by proof and facts.** The believer has **everything to gain and nothing to lose**. The Christian faith is not founded on wishful thinking or blind acceptance of truth, but rather on a tremendous body of real objective evidence." (Blick, E., 1986, Creation and Noah's Ark, Southwest Radio Church booklet, 24 pp.)

"If the intelligent design people are right God isn't hidden. We may be able to encounter God through science...if we have the freedom to go there. If you believe in God, and if you believe there's an intrinsic order in the universe, and you believe that it is the role of science to try to pursue and to understand better that order you will be ostracized. I believe the science gives us one perspective on the world and our religious insight gives us another insight on the world – and by putting the two together we'll see more deeply and more truly." (Stein, B., 2008, Expelled – No Intelligence Allowed)

God and His Word are fundamental to a morally healthy and progressive science, culture and nation. The roots of modern civilization are rotting away because of lies and deception. The influence of Darwin's mantra, 'time, time, give us more time,' is a premeditated excuse for promoting the false theory of evolution and the rejection of God's revealed truth. Consider the following statements:

> "I can prove God statistically. Take the human body alone --- the chance that all the functions of the individual would just happen is a statistical monstrosity." (Dr. George Gallup, director of the Gallup Poll, *in* Blick, E., 1986)

> "To me it is unthinkable that a real atheist could be a scientist." (Physicist Dr. Robert Milliken, a Nobel Prize winner) (Ibid)

> "I have no hesitation in saying that at least 90 percent of astronomers have reached the conclusion that the universe is not the result of blind law, but is regulated by a great intelligence." (Dr. C. A. Chant, professor of Astrophysics at Toronto University) (Ibid)

Our modern culture and institutions are following a path of social and spiritual entropy. The only force that can resist this decay is the living Word of God which, when applied by the Spirit of God can reverse social decline and ultimate destruction. No wonder our young people are adrift and losing their sense of the meaning of life, and turning to drugs and suicide. We have taught them to be this way by taking God out of their lives. This path is to our own personal and collective danger and ultimate destruction as a nation.

> "It's either back to the jungle, or back to the Bible." (Ruckman, Pastor P. S.)

> *"It is the spirit that quickeneth; the flesh profiteth nothing: the words that I speak unto you, they are spirit, and they are life."* (John 6:63)

Evolutionary philosophy is destroying our society today by teaching moral relativism and the idea we that have come from, and are going, nowhere. It is a doctrine without substance and without hope. The Bible makes many references to hell and the consequences of rejecting God. Most people follow lies into the fiery abyss which lies in the lower, partially melted upper crust and earth's mantle and deeper in its super-heated mantle and liquid outer core. Temperatures in hell are in the thousands of degrees! There is a lowest hell, no doubt deep within the earth.

> *"Enter ye in at the strait gate: for wide is the gate, and broad is the way, that leadeth to destruction (hell), and many there be which go in thereat.* (Matthew 7:13)

Geochronology and its various methods, collectively called radiometric 'dating,' are philosophically biased by Darwinian evolutionary theory. They are dependent upon unrealistic assumptions that yield dates that are questionable and unreliable at best. **Table 5** (below) has been assembled for the interested reader from a *Critique of Radiometric Dating (1973)*, *Evolution's Achilles' Heels (2014)* and *Contested Bones* (2017). It is included for the interested student. Slusher's book describes the mathematical formulae used in the radiometric 'dating' methods to arrive at the millions and billions of year's dates for geological processes, the fossil record and the 'age' of the earth. Carbon-14 dates concern more 'recent' time periods.

| 'DATING' METHOD | ASSUMPTIONS | WEAKNESS OF 'DATING' METHOD | IS THE 'DATING' METHOD RELIABLE? |
|---|---|---|---|
| | 1. no daughter element in rock when formed | | |
| | 2. parent element's decay rate constant over time | | |
| | 3. rock has remained a closed system since formed | | |
| U - Th - Pb "Clocks" | 1, 2 and 3 must all be true or methods not reliable | Changes in temp. or pressure, increase of cosmic ray collisions- decay of earth's | Measurements show decay rate NOT constant in time, **$Po^{218}$ (half-life = 3 min.)** in |
| | All assumptions are unknowable - therefore all | magnetic field; radii in pleochroic haloes vary in same nuclear | pleochroic haloes widespread indicating instantaneous fiat |
| | methods are unreliable and untrustworthy in many **cases.** (Dr. Jim Mason, McMaster U.) | material in same matrix = variable decay constants; earth's early crust & solar system | creation of earth & its crust (Gen. 1:1) |
| Three "Clocks" | | (incl. meteorites) not homogeneous, | Cook's Q time index ($Pb^{206}/Pb^{207}$) calculated the alleged ages of the |
| $U^{238}$ decays to $Pb^{206}$ + 8 He | Final & initial concentrations of U & Th in sample must be known; assume eons | Initial $U_o$ & $Th_o$ guessed, including primordial lead ($Pb_o$); not all $Pb^{206}$, $Pb^{207}$, | various rocks for various methods and 500 widespread samples of different 'geological |
| $U^{235}$ decays to $Pb^{207}$ + 7 He | of evolution which guides their dating of geologic events; various methods used | $Pb^{208}$ & $He^4$ due to decay - **He** escapes from rocks into atmosphere, **He in 1 1/2 b y old** Zircon xls | ages' - found no systematic variation at all anywhere; therefore, lead |

| | | | |
|---|---|---|---|
| | | | isotope method useless as a time clock |
| $Th^{232}$ decays to $Pb^{208}$ + 6 He | U / Th / Pb Method prone to violating Assumption 3 | NOT POSSIBLE! Soluble U. salts carried from rocks into sea; U & Th earth's surface by | **OR** the ages of the rocks are small = **young earth**; correction factor for neutron reactions |
| | | volcanism; $Pb^{208}/Th^{232}$ standard clock gives substantially greater ages than the other 2 | takes ages of hundreds of millions of years and nearly 2 billion years to nearly zero; Cook's |
| | | clocks - not decay but neutron reactions producing changes in the isotopic ratios | P-ratios calculated for many samples = zero to infinity showing U - Th - Pb" Clocks" either not |
| | | causing the 'long ages' of evolutionary theory, Cook - neutron flux | time clocks **OR** telling a time too short to be measurable = young |
| | | causes large changes in $N^{14}/N^{15}$ - could also in $Pb^{206}/Pb^{207}$ therefore | earth, crust formed very rapidly - with haloes. |
| | | upsetting this time clock from billions to a few thousand years; | "Open system" behavior due to groundwater transportation, etc. |
| | | Hypotheses on origin of earth's crust are the basis for initial amts. of $U_o$ & $Th_o$ | |
| | | Moon and earth rocks contain radioactive minerals with **very short half-lives.** | |
| $K^{40}$ - $Ar^{40}$ "Clock" | Commonly used for igneous material (granite, basalt & ash); | Highly discordant ages in areas of tremendous tectonic activity; ages | **Huge ages** being obtained by $K^{40}$ - $Ar^{40}$ "clock" for surface rocks |
| | 'clock' starts when the material cools or | too high compared to U - Th - Pb ages: arbitrary | **due to diffusion** of $Ar^{40}$ from deep in crust; difficulty |

| | | | |
|---|---|---|---|
| | crystallizes - assume no Argon when 'clock' | branching ratio taken to get dates | determining decay constants... |
| | starts; Need to know $K^{40}$ amount accurately; no adding of $Ar^{40}$ into mineral@ | to match them; far too much $Ar^{40}$ in earth for decay - 99.6% of total $Ar^{40}$ in atmosphere | branching ratios used as semi-empirical, adjustable constant that is manipulated instead |
| | crystallization or leak of $Ar^{40}$ after crystallization; system | -100 X that generated by radioactive decay over '4.5 by age' of | |
| | must be closed for $K^{40}$ & $Ar^{40}$ since crystallization; | earth ...therefore must have been large amount of $Ar^{40}$ in the | of using an accurate half-life for $K^{40}$; actual branching ratio not used |
| | relation between data & specific geological event must be known | beginning; $Ar^{40}$ diffuses from mineral to mineral very easily - | - instead a small ratio is chosen in an effort to match with U - Th - Pb |
| | Method violates Assumption 1 | leaking from deep in earth to surface where it collects...**excess $Ar^{40}$ makes rocks at** | dates...**"juggling"** the data to fit the Darwinian narrative or worldview; |
| | | **surface appear older**; some rocks hold $Ar^{40}$ stronger than others & appear older; | argon "outgassing" at crystallization or cooling not 100% effective, leading to excess argon |
| | | many rocks inherit $Ar^{40}$ from magma - **old ages obtained from** | and greatly inflated ages; |
| | | **very recent lava flows**, $Ar^{40}$ can diffuse into minerals at low pressures; $K^{40}$ is very | |
| | | mobile under leaching...can move ages to tremendously high values; | |
| | | In complex geologic history-rocks mutually contaminating K-bearing minerals. | |

| | | | |
|---|---|---|---|
| $Rb^{87}$ - $Sr^{87}$ "Clock" | Unrealistic assumptions | Utterly impossible to determine initial concentration of $Sr^{87}$ atoms, | Assumptions make it not a "clock" at all; **much "juggling"** of numbers & equations to get |
| | Decay constant uncertain...half-life = 49.9 b. y. | $Sr^{87}$ is 10X more abundant than if formed by $Rb^{87}$ decay over 5 b. y. - most $Sr^{87}$ | results in agreement with the U - Th - Pb "clocks," **to fit Darwinian concepts**; |
| | | is non-radiogenic, diffusion of $Sr^{87}$ completely ignored, even say | ALL values in ALL "clocks" are made to give values that fit the Darwinian evolutionist's |
| | Method violates Assumptions 1 & 3 | whole rock can be closed to diffusion BUT individual minerals open; whole rock ages | preconceived notions about the age of the earth and ages of geological events; |
| | | have many serious faults...practically all sample may be | results are MADE to give similar ages...ANY age that is desirable is |
| | | non-radiogenic $Sr^{87}$ introducing large error in measurements; | accepted – undesirable ages are rejected; it is certain that none of the |
| | | Isochron technique demands 1. same initial $Sr^{87}/Sr^{86}$, 2. samples same age & | rocks are closed systems; there is no way to correct for natural isotopic variation as no |
| | | 3. closed system, - if contamination and diffusion - how do we decide ages? **IF** age is | way to determine it; Therefore $Rb^{87}$ - $Sr^{87}$ "Clock" is USELESS. |
| | | too high or too low it is CORRECTED to the U - Th - Pb "Clock" | |

| | | | |
|---|---|---|---|
| | | Because $Sr^{87}$ disappears often by ion exchange processes. | |
| $C^{14}$ "Clock" | $C^{14}$ in atmosphere exchanged continually into organism while it lives, when it dies the | Standard date of 1950 used to work back from because of nuclear bomb testing & burning | No detectable Carbon-14 should remain in any biological remains after about 100,000 years. |
| | exchange stops & the $C^{14}$ decays to $C^{12}$ with a constant half-life of 5,760 years; assume | fossil fuels changed the atmosphere's $C^{14}/C^{12}$(ratio). | Therefore, $C^{14}$ shows how 'young' things are; evolution's assumption of a standard |
| | standard concentration in atmosphere...with same atmospheric conditions in the past, | 1. Vapor canopy, 2. Shielding by stronger magnetic field - both in the past; | concentration is wrong; $C^{14}$ is found in coals, fossils, fossil fuels and diamonds dated millions |
| | **BUT** T. G. Barnes indicates large variation in $C^{14}$ concentration in the | 1. Based upon Biblical record in Genesis 1 - waters above the firmament shielded | or billions of years old - can't be – **Something is wrong here!!** |
| | atmosphere over time...less in past; Therefore $C^{14}$ decay rate is NOT a constant, Less $(C^{14})_o$ and larger | earth from cosmic radiation making lower $C^{14}$ and greater apparent ages compared to standard, | $C^{14}$ is too unstable to last that long! Therefore, decay rate not **predictable** (J. L. Anderson); 'Old earth' |
| | apparent age of the sample, $C^{14}$ and other radioactive isotopes' decay rates may have | 2. Earth's main magnetic field - decreasing with time at a very rapid - | model means $C^{14}$ production due to cosmic radiation should = rate of decay - i.e. |
| | varied with time due to unknown conditions. | (?) - exponential rate (Barnes and others); half-life of the magnetic field strength | Equilibrium – **BUT** there is no equilibrium...24% or more $C^{14}$ is being produced than is |
| | **All coal beds in all formations worldwide have same amount of $C^{14}$ and give same age | is 1,400 yr. - after 9,800 yr. down to1% of original strength; This FIELD shields earth's | decaying...Calculate beginning of radiocarbon in atmosphere back to the |

| | | | |
|---|---|---|---|
| | worldwide: Therefore, all coals were laid down in the recent past. | organisms from cosmic rays; working back in time with Joule heating from currents in earth's | time of Flood (4500 years ago) when whole atmosphere fluxed of carbon & carbon locked |
| | Possibly violates Assumptions 1 - 3 | core would separate core and mantle after 20,000 yr. and destroy the whole earth in one | out of all organic domains by sudden deposition and all non-aquatic species being on |
| | | million years, Strength of magnetic field gives absolute maximum age | the Ark; Method very QUESTIONABLE because of likely changes in rate |
| | | **of the earth as 10,000 years** - less $C^{14}$ produced due to less cosmic radiation | of production of $C^{14}$ in the past and because of unknown decay rates in the past; failure of the |
| | | passing through the magnetic field changes $(C^{14})_0$ in the time equation very | equilibrium model and contamination render this method incorrect. |
| | | radically, and therefore the **ages** of artifacts, archeological artifacts and sites & associated | |
| | | geological events would be **too large**; primordial $N^{14}_0$ in atmosphere unknown | |
| | | - NB in production of $C^{14}$ , **$C^{14}$ ubiquitous in the fossil record** | |

**Table 5**

From: Slusher, 1973, Critique of Radiometric Dating Methods; Mason, 2014, Evolution's Achilles' Heels; Rupe & Sanford, 2017, Contested Bones

Before the advent of radiometric 'dating,' there was only a relative chronology, "a chronology without years," according to the British geologist Arthur Holmes. He wrote the following:

"Until the discovery of radioactivity, geologists were in the same position as a historian who knew, for example, that the Roman invasion of Britain was followed by the Norman Conquest, and that both of these events occurred before the Battle of Waterloo, but who could not find any record of the dates of these or any of the other great events of history." He emphasized that radioactivity provides a way of establishing an absolute chronology (i.e. in years)." (Holmes, A., 1965 edition, Principles of Physical Geology, p. 346)

Something is seriously wrong with the radiometric 'dating' method as a whole. No college or university student will be told this by his professor. They are kept in the dark that is likely all wrong.

"Behind the very sophisticated technologies that are used to date samples, are many layers of questionable assumptions. They tell us precisely about its isotopic composition – but NOT its age. Precision is not the same as accuracy. Physically precise measurements taken in the present do not automatically translate into correct dating of past events. These methods routinely yield conflicting ages. Those data that do not agree with the expected or desired age...are very often discarded (because) that date is problematic for the (e.g., ape-to-man) narrative. It is entirely feasible to accurately correlate stratigraphic sequences using **relative dating methods** (faunal or paleo-magnetic reversal correlations), yet still obtain an **absolute age** (a radioisotope age) that is absolutely wrong. Selective use of data, whether it is deliberate or passive, is bad science." (Rupe, C., and Sanford, J., 2017, Contested Bones, pp. 270-271)

The presence of the unstable $C^{14}$ isotope in rocks supposedly millions or billions of years old, as 'dated' by other radioactive "clocks" is enough evidence to warn that geochronology is invalid and needs to be set aside as an age indicator. Biblical chronology fits the observed data far better, though to the minds of finite men it seems unreasonable and preposterous.

The earth's electric and magnetic fields are generated through the 'dynamo effect,' emanating from the earth's solid iron inner core and the liquid iron-nickel outer core and adjoining ductile, iron mineral rich mantle rock. Circulating currents of charged particles in the core induce the earth's magnetic field which Thomas Barnes, in 1971, found to be undergoing (?) exponential decay with a half-life of 1400 years. After 7 half-lives or 9,800 years, the field would lose over 99% of its original strength. Joule heat energy caused by currents in the core build up rapidly over time. This heat would separate the core and mantle by 20,000 years B.P. and, in one million years, being 3 X $10^{215}$ tesla, would totally destroy the whole earth. (Slusher, H., 1973, Critique of Radiometric Dating, pp. 36-37) The earth's electrical field must have been affected by changes in the magnetic field as the two are interrelated. Radiometric age dates would have been compromised by electromagnetic entropy. Dr. Donald Chittick, a physical chemist, stated in a lecture tape that a change of $1/10^{th}$ of one percent in the earth's electrical field would reduce the calculated age date for the Uranium/Lead decay series from 4 ½ billion years to less than one second. Higher radioactive decay rates and shorter isotope half-lives in the past could have produced excess daughter elements and huge ages using modern assumptions. This point alone calls into serious doubt the whole Darwinian age narrative.

Professor Barnes (U. of Texas at El Paso) also concluded the following based upon the decay of the earth's magnetic field:

> "20,000 years is an absolute maximum for the age of the earth and 10,000 years is a far more reasonable value." (Slusher, H., 1973, Critique of Radiometric Dating, ICR Technical Monograph No. 2, p. 37)

A careful examination of Genesis chapters one-through-eleven permits us to reconstruct early earth history right back to, and including, the Early Precambrian **(Figure 1)**. The Pre-Flood human genealogies from Adam to Methuselah define earth history from creation to the Flood (1656 A.C./2348 B.C.). Noah's life bridged the Flood and Post-Flood eras. The Post-Flood genealogies encompass the "days of Peleg" when the earth was divided, and onward to Abraham and his descendants. These are specific dates given in years. The present work correlates this part of the Biblical time scale to the Mesozoic and Cenozoic eras as shown in the preceding chapters **(Figures 1** and **2)**. The Bible is giving us the true picture of geology and we need to honor it. The author spent nearly six years in University without ever questioning the uniformitarian message. He was ignorant of the Bible's teaching until after he was saved in 1981. He asserts that a new approach is needed to free us from the harmful effects of Darwinian philosophy, both individually and as a society, and bring us back to faith in God's Word.

**Fit science to the Bible, and not the Bible to science, to find the true answers.** It is a matter of faith in the God of the Bible or faith in the man, Charles Darwin...a 'no-brainer.' Biblical chronology will be the critical factor in finding ultimate answers in earth science. It will lead us to the correct interpretation of the age of the earth and the unification of the physical laws governing our earth and the universe. It also clears away the fallacies of radiometric dating and evolution that hinder our finding correct answers in science and other fields of study. It is not easy to go against the flow and oppose the popular consensus in this day and age. But it is necessary if we are to progress not just materially, but most importantly, morally and spiritually as a free democratic society.

> "Creationists have to pay the price of academic ridicule and occasional personal attacks, but these are nothing compared to the riches of knowledge and wisdom that are ours through Christ! I only wish that more scientists, science teachers and science students could share the joy and challenge of looking at God's world through God's eyes." (Parker, G., 2008, From Evolution to Creation: A Personal Testimony)

The Scriptures give the definitive reason for all things, whether scientific, social or personal. You can find eternal salvation in the Word of God and there is no greater discovery than that! To know the true God who made it all is the greatest blessing and source of freedom a scientist or non-scientist could ever receive.

Eternal life is found by accepting Jesus Christ as your Lord and Savior. Job was a man of knowledge with impeccable character and integrity. Yet he rejoiced to know the Lord as his personal Savior. The story of his suffering and testimony of faith are summarized in **Appendix 1**.

# WHAT IS THE EVOLUTION DEBATE ALL ABOUT??

The Scriptures give the definitive reason for why mankind is replacing our traditional Judeo-Christian culture with new philosophies and seeking to remake the world into a Utopia or 'perfect' society. The evolution debate is only a part of the picture, albeit not a small part. 'Advocacy science' is the rule in academia today based upon a narrative, paradigm, worldview, ideology of Darwinian/Marxist bias. It is promoted by 'Advocacy journalism' by the mainstream media by the same methods.

> *"The kings of the earth set themselves, and the rulers take counsel together, against the LORD, and against his anointed, saying, Let us break their bands asunder, and cast away their cords from us."* (Psalm 2:2-3)

Saul Alinsky, the radical leftist professor from the 1960s and 70s, put it in a nutshell. He authored *Rules for Radicals (1971)*, the guidebook for Antifa, and all elements of the radical left, in 2021. He is what he wrote:

> **"THE ISSUE IS NEVER THE ISSUE; THE ISSUE IS ALWAYS THE REVOLUTION."**
>
> "In paleoanthropology, the fossil evidence has always been interpreted in light of the evolutionary view of human history. The ape-to-man story did not arise by scientific observations; it arose as a philosophically driven speculation, based on Darwin's writings. The paleo-community is confused because they are interpreting the fossils in light of the flawed ideological presupposition that the Darwinian mechanism explains everything, even us. (It) acknowledges that the hominin fossil record does not reflect an ape-to-man progression because there appears to be a clear separation between the ape and human types. There is branching within each group but no fossils connecting the groups." (yet) "In the paleo-community there remains an unconditional commitment to the basic Darwinian paradigm, and there is an unwavering fidelity to the basic ape-to-man narrative...the evidence is consistently interpreted in light of the paradigm. Our worldview (all of us) colors how we see everything." (Rupe, C., and Sanford, J., 2017, Contested Bones, pp. 340-342, 351)

The reason it is so difficult to debate and refute issues like evolution with secular science is that the real issue is not about evolution at all; but it is all about – THE REVOLUTION – mankind's revolution against the LORD, AND HIS ANOINTED, the Lord Jesus Christ, God's only begotten Son (Psalm 2:1-3). Underlying this revolution is Satan's war against God. He works through unregenerate (unsaved) humanity. The same condition applies to the ape-to-man debate (above), carbon 'footprint' and global warming, radiometric dating and the age of the earth, racial-gender debate (Critical Race Theory) and intersectionality, abortion, capital punishment, euthanasia, feminism and every other area of scientific and social conflict in the world today. Nor is the issue about the COVID-19 'Planned-demic' and planned mass-vaccination import. It is all about the REVOLUTION; the Darwinian socialist-communist revolution, which is about POWER! – Man against God, with Satan working behind the scenes! Even if every valid reason under the sun could be successfully debated against any or all of these points of contention, including Darwinian or any other form of evolution, the issue would still remain the REVOLUTION. Jesus Christ drew the same comparison in Luke 16 regarding personal salvation as the rich man in hell pleaded with Abraham in paradise.

> *"And he said, Nay, father Abraham: but if one went unto them from the dead, they will repent. And he said unto him, If they hear not Moses and the prophets, neither will they be persuaded, though one rose from the dead."* (Luke 16:30-31)

> "The Darwinian revolution marked the end of the age of belief in the design argument among scientists. Scientists in Darwin's day knew that this revolution was upon them. Botanist and phrenologist H. C. Watson wrote to Darwin on November 21, 1859, informing him that **Darwin was the "greatest Revolutionist in natural history of this century, if not of all centuries."** Oxford University professor of the history of science I. B. Cohen concluded: "**Darwinian revolution** was probably the most significant revolution that has ever occurred in the sciences, because its effects and influences were significant in many different areas of thought and belief. The consequences of this revolution was a systematic rethinking of the nature of the world, of man, and of human institutions...This event, a declaration of revolution in a formal scientific publication, appears to be without parallel in the history of science." (Bergman, J., The Dark Side of Charles Darwin, p. 48)

**Charles Darwin** revolted against God as Creator, by denying His Word in *On the Origin of Species (1859)*, thereby destroying God's place of eminence in academia. He forfeited his soul in doing so. **Karl Marx** denied God as Lord of lords and King of Kings and sought to tear down Western civilization's socio-economic and political system in *The Communist Manifesto (1848)* and *Das Kapital (3 Vol., 1867-94)*. **Fenton John Anthony Hort** tore the Traditional Text of the Holy Scriptures from the 19th and 20th Century churches with the corrupt *Critical Greek Text (1881)* and its product, *The English Revised Version (1883)*, leading to the proliferation of modern, corrupt Bible versions, and pushing an already weakening church into full apostasy. The Traditional Hebrew, Greek and Aramaic Text continues to be under attack from various sources to the present day. This three-pronged attack has knocked the legs out from under the Bible-believing Christian churches, and Judeo-Christian Free Democracy in the Western world. As a result, Western society is rapidly collapsing and morphing into an international radical, socialist-communist totalitarian dictatorship. Each of these attacks involved an adherence to Darwinian evolution in one form or another.

> "I am haunted by a conviction that the *nihilistic philosophy which so-called educated opinion chose to adopt following the publication of *On the Origin of Species* committed mankind to a course of automatic self-destruction. A doomsday was then set ticking." (Ferrell, V., The Evolution Handbook, 2001, quoting Astrophysicist Sir Fred Hoyle, 1983, p. 802)

* **nihilism** – violent **revolution** aiming to destroy all existing institutions, anarchy (Winston Dictionary, College Edition, 1946)

> "Darwin knew that to "murder" God he had to come up with a naturalist theory of the origin of life. In this he was enormously successful, and managed to convert the larger part of the scientific community and much of the rest of the world to his naturalistic theory of origins and, as a result, "destroyed the strongest evidence left in the nineteenth century for the existence of a deity." In the minds of many scientists, Darwin had murdered God. Darwin did this with a theory that lacked substantial scientific evidence and, in the past century and a half, has become increasingly difficult to defend scientifically, especially after the advent of the DNA molecular revolution and the enormous fossil finds that document stasis (stoppage), not cell to human evolution. **Darwin's goal was very clear: 'The main purpose of Darwinism was to drive every last trace of an incredible God from biology...replacing the old God with an even more incredible deity – omnipotent chance.'**...if the argument from design was dead (so was) the existence of a personal god, free will, life after death, immutable moral laws, and ultimate meaning in life." (Bergman, J., 2011, The Dark Side of Charles Darwin, pp. 40-41)

Darwin knew that by "murdering" God he was murdering Western civilization and culture as well by robbing it of faith in the Word of God (the Bible). The fruit of his revolution contributed to the apostasy of the church. And he did it all with a great lie. The Bible foretold of such deception near the end of the church age, just before the rapture of the saved children of God (the Christians), as the world descended into moral **chaos** and the reign of a great totalitarian dictator, the Antichrist.

> *"Let no man deceive you by any means: for that day (the rapture) shall not come except there come a falling away (apostasy) first, and that man of sin (the Antichrist) be revealed, the son of perdition. Even him, whose coming is after the working of Satan with all power and signs and lying wonders, And with all deceivableness of unrighteousness in them that perish; because they received not the love of the truth, that they might be saved.* ***And for this cause God shall send them strong delusion, that they should believe a lie:*** (2 Thessalonians 2:3, 9-11)

Darwinian evolution has metamorphosed into a doomsday scenario in 2021. We have only to look at the COVID-19 'Planned-demic' and the response worldwide. This man-made pestilence is ushering in a worldwide loss of personal freedoms in the Western democracies. Underlying this orchestrated attack is the government-mandated propaganda toward fear-driven lockdowns and mass vaccination of millions with untested gene therapy "vaccines." Millions of souls are being injected with experimental, metal nano-technologies that can be turned on-and-off, and are producing many bizarre and dangerous side-effects on the unwitting recipients.

Dr. Joseph Mercola wrote on March 31, 2021, "Can mRNA Gene Therapy Jabs Permanently Alter Your DNA?"

"The mRNA of retroviruses have the ability to transcribe into your DNA, so why not COVID-19 vaccine mRNA? Study by MIT and Harvard scientists demonstrates that segments of RNA from SARS-CoV-2 are reverse-transcribing into the human genome, likely becoming a permanent fixture in human DNA. Currently, mRNA is considered a gene therapy product by the FDA. It is only designed to lessen symptoms, not prevent infection and spread of COVID-19. In a 2017 TED Talk, Dr. Tal Zaks, chief medical officer of Moderna, describes the company's mRNA vaccines as "information technology," and likens mRNA to your body's operating system. As such, mRNA injections are human "software updates," thereby ushering in **transhumanism**. The synthetic mRNA "vaccines" won't degrade but keep on producing spike proteins. How long? No one knows because it has never been tested. The pandemic allowed vaccine makers to sneak mRNA gene therapy under the proverbial radar so they don't have to conduct more stringent gene therapy testing. Instead, they were handed the global population for the largest testing imaginable, and all without liability."

"Pure and simple, this is unvarnished, raw transhumanism – scientists think they can improve on a person's God-given genetic makeup...(they) truly believe that the human body is nothing more than a machine that can be hacked into and reordered according to some program's instruction. Who's to say they won't correct one problem and create something far worse?" (Patrick Wood in Technocracy News) "The COVID-19 pandemic was manufactured by the world's elites as part of a plan to globally advance **'transhumanism,'** the fusion of human beings with technology in an attempt to alter human nature itself and create a superhuman being and an 'earthly paradise...the Fourth Industrial Revolution.' (It) requires the concentration of political and economic power in the hands of a global elite and the dependence of the people upon the state." (Miklos Lukacs, research professor of science and technology policy – Peruvian University San Martin de Porres, in Life Site News, November 10, 2020) Contrary to what some scientists believe, we are not machines...or putty that can be modified or molded to our taste and our desire by rejecting those limits nature or God have placed on us. We are human beings with bodies, souls and free wills. Anyone who tries to mandate an acceptance of an experimental gene-altering treatment is going against the International Nuremberg Codes, which require informed consent of any experimental treatment."

This whole "transhumanism" agenda is Darwinian evolution at its worst, reaching its depressing climax. Man is attempting to evolve into "God," as he rebels against his Creator. He will destroy himself in the process, and millions of innocent lives will be lost through irresponsible actions by our governments aligning with Big Pharma and its squads of mRNA vaccine scientists. The Canadian Federal and Provincial governments are pushing these vaccines on the citizens through the left-wing, mainstream media in 2021. Note the following article by Stephanie Babych, **'Milestone' for Alberta – Province expands COVID-19 vaccine eligibility to everyone age 12 and up**, in the May 6, 2021, Calgary Sun newspaper.

"All Albertans age 12 and over will be eligible to receive a COVID-19 vaccine as soon as Monday (May 10), Premier Jason Kenny announced Wednesday...bookings for those aged 12 to 29 will open Monday. By shifting to

Phase 3 of the province's vaccine strategy, another 3.8 million people will become eligible. Health Canada approved the Pfizer-BioN-Tech vaccine for children 12 and older."

No wonder people are running to get their "jab" or shot! The media has been hyping the COVID statistics incessantly creating a culture of fear and anxiety in the general population for over a year. This brainwashing has captured the minds of our leaders and they have moved the masses to rush into the untested and uncharted waters of "gene therapy." All but a few will go for it! The front page of the May 10, 2021 Calgary Sun reads, **"Vax shots now open to Albertans 12 & older >>page 4 COME ONE, COME ALL"** Never before have the masses as a whole been so well prepared, well-conditioned and willing to actually WANT an untried and untested "vaccine" (gene therapy) on this scale as with the COVID-19 "Planned-demic." **Something is dreadfully wrong in this whole thing!**

This "Great Reset" **revolution** will climax in a worldwide dictator (the Antichrist) taking control of all nations ushering in the Great Tribulation prophesied in the Bible. The Church (the saved) will be raptured before this happens. The Antichrist will rule with a murderous, materialist Marxist-Darwinian ideology as his modus operandi. He is foretold in many books of the Bible, most notably Daniel and Revelation. The false theory of evolution has helped prepare the world to accept this leader who will "honour the God of forces." He will exalt the material world and its natural forces, outlaw worship of the true God, and focus all worship toward himself. Charles Darwin was one of his predecessors and helped prepare the way before him. This one-world leader is called the Beast in Scripture and is to be indwelt by Satan. He will soon emerge on the world stage. All who take his mark and worship him will go to the eternal lake of fire.

> *"And the king shall do according to his will; and he shall exalt himself, and magnify himself above every god, and shall speak marvelous things against the God of gods…for he shall magnify himself above all. But in his estate shall he honour the God of forces…"* (Daniel 11:36-38 pt.)

A book such as the one you have just read, whether in whole or in part, will persuade very few people to change their position scientifically or spiritually. The author hopes that it will help some to question their secular beliefs and turn to the Bible and begin reading it with an open mind. Hopefully, out of that effort, even a few souls will be saved and reconciled to their Maker before it is too late. Remember, if you wish to revolt against God as Darwin did, do you expect to win? It is after all Almighty God that you are fighting against. And He loved you enough to send His only begotten Son, Jesus Christ, the Creator, to die on the cross for your sin.

> ***"For God so loved the world, that he gave his only begotten Son, that whosoever believeth in him should not perish, but have everlasting life."***
> (John 3:16)

# LIST OF REFERENCES


Aharoni, E., 1966, Oil and Gas Prospects of Kurnub Group (Lower Cretaceous) in southern Israel AAPG Bulletin, vol. 50, no. 11.

Armitage, M. and Anderson, K., 2013, Soft sheets of fibrillary bone from a fossil of the supraorbital horn of the dinosaur *Triceratops horridus*, Elsevier, Acta Histochemica 115, pp. 603-608

Arnaud, B., 2000, Burial Practices of the Maraca Indians: Archeology Magazine, May-June issue

Authorized Version of the Bible, 1611, Cambridge University Press, London

Bergman, J., 2011, The Dark Side of Charles Darwin: A Critical Analysis of an Icon of Science, Master Books, 270 pp.

Bethune, B., 2001, Mystery of the First North Americans: Maclean's Magazine, March 19 issue

Blick, E., 1986, Creation and Noah's Ark, Southwest Radio Church booklet – B-567, 24 pp.

Buday, T., 1980, The Regional Geology of Iraq: The State Organization for Minerals, Baghdad

Crawford, F., 1972, Facies and Depositional Environments in the Middle Devonian Slave Point and Fort Vermillion Formations of Northern Alberta, MSc. Thesis, U. of Calgary

Crawford, F., ed, 1972, Arenaceous Deposits: Sedimentation and Diagenesis, Department of Extension, University of Alberta, 286 pp.

Dixon, D. et al, 1988, Mac Millan Illustrated Encyclopedia of Dinosaurs and Prehistoric Animals, Mac Millan Publishing Company, New York

Douglas, R., 1969, Geology and Economic Minerals of Canada

Eberth, D., 1994, Tectonics and Taphonomy: Why does Alberta have so many dinosaurs? CSPG Reservoir Abstract, vol. 21, no. 2

Evolution's Achilles' Heels – 15 PhD scientists explain evolution's fatal flaws, 2014, DVD format, Creation Ministries International

Ferrell, V., 2001, The Evolution Handbook, 992 pp.

Geocanada 2000, Ray Price Symposium, concluding comments by Dr. Ray Price, University of Calgary

Helton, D., 2021, Evolution: Another False Religion of Humanism, The Old Paths Publications Inc.

Holmes, A., 1964, Principles of Physical Geology: Thomas Nelson and Sons Ltd., London, 1288 pp. (1965 ed. quoted from Slusher, H.)

Wigoder, G., General Editor, 1986, Illustrated Dictionary and Concordance of the Bible, GG The Jerusalem Publishing House, 1070 pp.

Keeley, M., 1991, The Jurassic System in Northern Egypt, Journal of Petroleum Geology, Scientific Press Ltd., Beaconsfield, England, pp. 49-64.

Linton, J., (date unknown), The Flood of Noah's Day, booklet published by the author

Longwell, C. and Flint, R., 1965, Introduction to Physical Geology: John Wiley and Sons, Inc., New York

Map of the Arctic Ocean Seafloor, 1989; National Geographic Society, Washington, D.C.

Mercola, J., "March 31, 2021, "Can mRNA Gene Therapy Jabs Permanently Alter Your DNA?" Mercola website

Parker, G., 2008, From Evolution to Creation: A Personal Testimony, Creation Ministries International booklet, 21 pp.

Romer, A., 1967, Vertebrate Paleontology, University of Chicago Press

Rupe, C., and Sanford, J., 2017, Contested Bones, FMS Publications, 368 pp.

Scofield, C., 1909, The Old Scofield Bible, Oxford University Press, 1530 pp.

Shell Oil Company, 1990, Geological Data Table, The Hague: Research Department

Shelton, J., 1966, Geology Illustrated: W. H. Freeman and Company, San Francisco

Stein, B., 2008, Expelled - No Intelligence Allowed, 2008, DVD format, Premise Media Corporation

Stewart, D., July 1992, Petrified footprints: a puzzling parade of Lower Permian beasts, Smithsonian, pp. 71-79

The Calgary Herald Newspaper, Calgary, Alberta, selected articles from various journalists

The Calgary Sun Newspaper, Calgary, Alberta, article for May 6, 2021

The Epoch Times Newspaper, Western Canada Edition, recent articles

The Prophetic Voice, 1940s, Monthly Bulletins of The Prophetic Bible Institute, Calgary, Alberta

The Winston Dictionary: College Edition, 1946, used for definitions

Turner, F., and Verhoogen, J., 1970, The Earth: An Introduction to Physical Geology, Holt, Rinehart and Winston Inc., New York

# LIST OF FIGURES

# LIST OF TABLES

# ABOUT THE AUTHOR

Frank Crawford was born in Pine Falls, Manitoba. He has called Calgary, Alberta, home since 1966. Frank graduated from the University of Calgary in 1969 and 1972 with BSc and MSc degrees in geology, specializing in Devonian carbonate sedimentation during his graduate studies. His Master's Thesis was based upon subsurface analysis of slabbed drill cores and chip samples using the fossils and rock textures to reconstruct depositional environments. He went on to work as a petroleum geologist. His experience as a Canadian domestic and international exploration geologist involved studying the stratigraphy, sedimentation and the structural history of many different kinds of sedimentary basins around the world. You are welcome to review his background as a petroleum exploration geologist on his LinkedIn profile. He is qualified to speak on the subject of geology, both in the secular realm and according to the teaching of the Christian scriptures.

Frank was respected professionally for his work both in Canada and internationally up until the time of his retirement in 2012. He retired as a member in good standing from APEGA (The Association of Professional Engineers and Geoscientists of Alberta).

Frank was able to bear a Christian witness in the oil industry for a long period of time. He came to a personal saving faith in the Lord Jesus Christ in 1981 while working in Calgary. He began reading and studying the Bible from that year onward. He started to integrate his secular geological knowledge with his Biblical studies after reading the Bible through for several years. This study resulted in the book you are reading, or have already finished reading. In these chapters he challenges the passive acceptance of evolution, Darwinian or otherwise, and exhorts the reader to consider the Biblical evidence for a young earth. He asserts that the Bible speaks authoritatively about major geological processes within the time frame of the Old Testament patriarchs, particularly in the Books of Job, Genesis and Psalms. From the Biblical and secular scientific evidence he concludes that the earth is thousands of years old and not millions or billions of years in the making.

Frank married in 1988 and together lives with his wife, Christian, in Calgary to the present. They serve together in a Baptist church and are involved in a mission project in the Central Philippines. Frank has helped to fundraise for his church's mission work after retiring.

Frank Crawford has taken the time to write in recent years bringing the Bible into the secular realm of politics, social concerns, education and science. He has written many Christian tracts on various subjects, and has just completed this work, his third book. He has decided to write this book as a contribution to society and to encourage his peers to re-examine their secular scientific and philosophical ideas and re-consider the claims in God's Word about the age of the earth, the origin of man and their personal accountability toward God and His Son, Jesus Christ.

Mr. Crawford would ask those with a science background or an interest in the subject of earth history, taught in the secular educational system, to examine open-mindedly what is written in this book. Frank does not claim to have all the answers on how the earth was formed and shaped. None of us do. But, in the interest of truth, which he believes the Bible to be, we might come to realize that God indeed formed and shaped all that is around us. He did not need millions of years to do it either. That should cause you to consider your relationship to the great God who did all these things so wonderfully and beyond our finite human minds to fully comprehend.

As the author of this book, I invite you to read the account of Job's sufferings in the Appendix and then to go on to examine the Gospel message after it. Your personal salvation is vastly more important than science or any scientific theories of origins, including creation science. That is why I have written this book – to try and give something back to my peers from my many years working as a petroleum exploration geologist. I hope to encourage you to consider that the Bible speaks accurately about every matter concerning the physical earth and man; and most importantly, about the purpose of life and the destiny of your never-dying soul. It is well worth taking the time to check these things out by reading the Bible; and I recommend the 1611 King James Version which is quoted in this book.

# APPENDIX 1

## THE SUFFERINGS OF JOB

There is a statue in Israel depicting the sufferings of Job. This is an appropriate piece of art for the Jewish people because they have suffered more than any other group through the centuries. Job's heroic sufferings were a source of inspiration and hope to these oft-persecuted people. God has preserved the story of this man in the Bible for the benefit of mankind. Reading it will help all persons put suffering in the proper perspective and see where God fits into the adversities of life. This is particularly relevant during the COVID-19 "Planned-demic." Let us look then at "The Sufferings of Job," from Job 2:3-11.

The COVID-19 "Planned-demic," as a pastor so recently coined the phrase, is a worldwide time of suffering unprecedented in scope. It is precisely at such a time people should be looking for real answers; not on the politically correct mainstream news networks, but in the Bible where the truth can be found. Long before God's Word came to completion the man Job personified the faith that overcomes the world. In his suffering he did not charge God foolishly but patiently endured great trials of affliction and saw God's blessing at the latter end.

The man Job embodies the perfect example for suffering persons. How does this man embody the perfect example for those who experience adversity in life?

### 1. Job's Basis of Suffering

There are many reasons for suffering in life, but there is only one firm basis for it, and that Job exemplified. He suffered for God's glory, although in his destitute condition he could not see it at the time.

> *"And the LORD said unto Satan, Hast thou considered my servant Job, That there is none like him in the earth, a perfect and an upright man, one that feareth God, and esheweth evil? and still he holdeth fast his integrity, although thou movedst me against him, to destroy him without a cause."* (Job 2:3)

Job was God's servant and the godliest person of his generation alive on the earth. He waited on the LORD and did His will in life. As a result Job was spiritually complete and a man whom God described as perfect and upright. He began by accepting the Lord as his Savior. He recognized his sin and need of salvation by faith in a redeemer who would pay for his sins. When at his lowest, he fled to God in whom he had put his trust.

> *"For I know that my redeemer liveth, and that he shall stand at the latter day upon the earth:"* (Job 19:25)

This is a confession of faith in Jesus Christ, looking forward to the coming of the Savior of the world more than two thousand years before it happened. He knew this redeemer was the one who would redeem his soul and forgive his sins. The word redeem means to purchase or pay for. Jesus Christ paid for the sin of the whole world with His shed blood, by His death on the cross. Until the Son of God came the Old Testament saints, like Job, offered animal sacrifices to cover, but not fully pay the cost for, their sins. Only the God-man, Jesus Christ, could do that.

> *"Forasmuch as ye know that ye were not redeemed with corruptible things, as silver and gold, from your vain conversation received by tradition from your fathers; But with the precious blood of Christ, as of a lamb without blemish and without spot:"* (I Peter 1:18-19)

As an upright man he walked "straight-footed" in the path that God had planned for his life.

This attitude was based on his fear of God, that is, a deep reverential respect for his Creator and Redeemer. His statement of faith embodies the needed blood atonement for sin, that is, an innocent substitute for the guilty sinner. Though Job was godly he was still a sinner and said,

> *"For thou writest bitter things against me, and makest me to possess the iniquities of my youth."* (Job 13:26)

When he or his children sinned Job was ready to offer the acceptable Old Testament sacrifice, a blood atonement that would temporarily cover sins until the redeemer would come.

> *"And it was so, when the days of their feasting were gone about, that Job sent and sanctified them, and rose up early in the morning, and offered burnt offerings according to the number of them all: for Job said, It may be that my sons have sinned, and cursed God in their hearts. Thus did Job continually."* (Job 1:3)

Thus Job cared for his family spiritually and showed leadership. Then tragedy struck through no fault of his own and he lost all of his substance, including his ten children. We know that this attack had come from Satan who hated Job and challenged God to allow His servant to suffer. All of this adversity came because Job loved God and served Him faithfully. Reading chapter 31 will persuade the reader of this man's sincerity and care for his fellow man. When God asked Satan, ***"Hast thou considered my servant Job...?"*** **(v. 8b)**, he answers in the affirmative and then begins to try and destroy God's man. God allows Satan to test His servant to prove his faith and love for his redeemer. Today, the Devil seeks to keep men from coming to salvation and if they become Christians he seeks to try and destroy them in any way that he can. He cannot their souls but tries to ruin their lives. The example of Job is an encouragement to believers who are suffering and a powerful testimony to souls in need of salvation.

## II Job's Baptism of Suffering (Figure below)

The firmest basis for enduring suffering is because of a love for God, as we see in Job's life. Sometimes, the greater a believer loves the Lord Jesus Christ the more trials they will experience. That is because Satan hates God, and man who is created in the image of God, though fallen and in need of salvation. Satan wants to lead people away from God, and even persuade them to curse Him. So began Job's baptism of suffering at the hand of his enemy, the Devil.

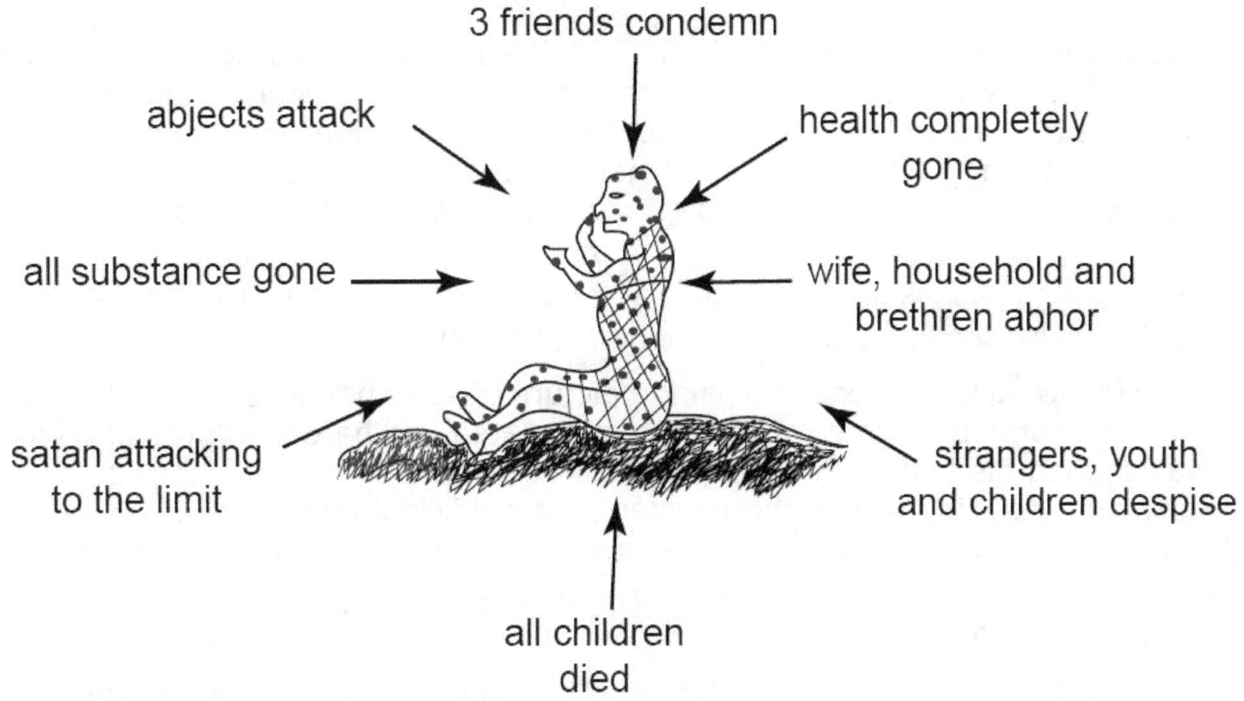


*"Though he slay me, yet will I trust in him: but I will maintain mine own ways before him."* (Job 13:15)

**Figure 1**

The sufferings of Job

**Figure 1** is a sketch depicting Job's baptism of suffering. Not only were his substance and his physical health destroyed, but also a host of other factors contributed to his misery.

Satan would make sure Job suffered. He knows man very well and employs every possible method to destroy him. First he takes away all of Job's substance, and his children. He attacks Job to the very limit allowed by God, killing all of his ten children, robbing every one of his livestock and killing his hired servants, all in one day! In twenty-four hours Job went from being the greatest of the men of the east to complete poverty. But he holds his faith though overwhelmed by the calamity.

Then Satan asks the LORD if he can attack Job physically, for that would be the best way to get him to curse his Maker. The Devil knows the weakness of man's flesh and capitalizes on it to overcome the spirit. And God gives him another opportunity to break Job.

*"And Satan answered the LORD, and said, Skin for skin, yea, all that a man hath will he give for his life."* (Job 2:4)

*"And the LORD said unto Satan, Behold, he is in thine hand; but save his life."* (Job 2:5)

Then Satan goes after his prey and strikes suddenly, covering Job from head to foot with horrible boils. Puss-filled sores break out upon his body from the crown of his head to the sole of his foot. They ooze out their infections in an odor of stench around the poor man. This disease did not come gradually but broke out almost instantaneously. Satan was attacking to the limit, just short of taking his victim's life.

*"So went Satan forth from the presence of the LORD, and smote Job with sore boils from the sole of his foot unto his crown."* (Job 2:7)

The following verse begins to paint a picture of Job's pitiful condition. He takes a broken piece of pottery to scrape off the coagulated and hardened puss and blood that was coating his body and oozing out of fresh sores. He sits in ashes as a sign of despair and possibly to use the powder as a medicinal coating over his broken flesh. The location for these ashes was a lonely dumping ground away from the city.

*"And he took him a potsherd to scrape himself withal; and he sat down among the ashes."* (Job 2:8)

Yet there was much more to his physical suffering. He was in a pitiful and destitute condition as demonstrated by the following verses:

*"My flesh is clothed with worms and clods of dust; my skin is broken and become loathsome."* (Job 7:5)

*"I have sewed sackcloth upon my skin, and defiled my horn in the dust."* (Job 16:15)

*"My bone cleaveth to my skin and to my flesh, and I am escaped with the skin of my teeth."* (Job 19:20)

*"By the great force of my disease is my garment changed: it bindeth me about as the collar of my coat."* (Job 30:18)

*"My skin is black upon me, and my bones are burned with heat."* (Job 30:30)

Job looked like the living dead in hell, his body infected and covered with boils, worms and caked dirt. Blackened skin and protruding bones attested to the force of the disease. So strong was it that his garment fused together with his flesh so the two became as one. His spittle came down out of his mouth, and he swallowed it again. Yet the picture is still not complete. Satan was oppressing him continually while in that pitiful state, trying to break Job's spirit and get him to curse God and end his life. The devil even used Job's wife to try and destroy him.

*"Then said his wife unto him, Dost thou still retain thine integrity? curse God, and die."* (Job 2:9)

His closest loved one tells him to get it all over with, curse God and then commit suicide. End it all Job but get your last lick at God by blaming Him for your misery. How many people today commit suicide and blame God for their problems. Job was wise enough not to do that. Faith in his redeemer eliminates any temptation to take things into his own hands. If you have serious problems in your life today turn to the Lord as Job did and you will find the strength to carry you through. It may be that you need to be saved. Let the suffering bring you into a right relationship with God. God's strong arm is always there to help you, even at rock bottom. Then call on Him in your distress. Jesus invites you to come to Him –

> *"Come unto me, all ye that labour and are heavy laden, and I will give you rest."* (Matthew 11:28)

## III Job's Badge of Suffering

Job suffered more than any man other than the Lord Jesus Christ. The Savior suffered greater anguish because He died for the sins of the whole world. Job did not bear our sins but he experienced Satan's full wrath short of death.

Job had to 'wear' his suffering, that is, to present it to a watching world and to heaven's angelic hosts. He wore the badge of suffering inscribed with one word, **"integrity"**. Throughout his ordeal he demonstrated a sound character showing honesty toward God and man. Job did not blame or condemn anyone for his problems but accepted them as coming from an all wise and knowing God. The LORD commended Job for his virtue.

> *"and still he holdeth fast his integrity, although thou movest me against him, to destroy him without cause."* (Job 2:3f-h)

Job's integrity showed toward his family and toward those in greatest need, namely the fatherless and widows. His benevolence was widely known and he was respected as no other man, until tragedy struck. Now in pitiful condition on the ash heap he answers his wife,

> *"Thou speakest as one of the foolish women speaketh. What? shall we receive good at the hand of God, and shall we not receive evil? In all this did not Job sin with his lips."* (Job 2:10)

To curse God and die would be playing the fool and acting as if there was no God. Job knew the LORD and would not be tempted to deny Him. The Scriptures say, **The fool hath said in his heart, *There is* no God.** *(Psalm 14:1a-b)* Job knew his redeemer and he had no intention of forgetting Him, even in great distress. He recognized and accepted God's sovereignty and control in his circumstances, though not understanding why he was suffering.

His personal integrity remained firm from the beginning of his sorrows until the end, though he was accosted and attacked by everyone. Job's physical afflictions were immeasurably heightened by human oppression as his family, friends, strangers and even little children turned against him. The man's emotional and spiritual distresses probably outweighed his physical suffering yet he said,

> *"til I die I will not remove mine integrity from me."* (Job 27:5b)

And from his broken lips come the words that have lifted hearts down through the millennia since that time so long ago. If Job can triumph through his faith, why can't we?

> *"Though he slay me, yet will I trust in him: but I will maintain mine own ways before him."* (Job 13:15)

> *"For I know that my redeemer liveth, and that he shall stand at the latter day upon the earth. And though after my skin worms destroy this body, yet in my flesh shall I see God:"* (Job 19:25-26)

In the end all Job had was God and all he needed was his Redeemer God. It is the same today. We may lose everything in life, even our life. But if we know the Lord Jesus Christ as our Savior, He is all we need for now and for eternity.

## Conclusion

The sufferings of Job are a great encouragement for all people. The basis for his calamity was love and obedience toward God. He had personal saving faith in his coming redeemer, Jesus Christ. He was baptized or immersed in tortuous adversity, losing everything but his life. Job was suffering all of this loss for the glory of God though he was a just man. He didn't know why at the time. Had he questioned God and cursed Him everything would have been lost, and there would be no Book of Job. His badge of integrity carried him through some of the greatest sufferings ever endured by a single man. Behind it all was the grace of God for which we can all be thankful today. Without that grace (unmerited favour) no one could be saved or gain victory over the trials of life. Job would be a good example for those suffering through COVID-19 in 2021. Can you say by faith,**" Though he slay me, yet will I trust in him?"**

"When nothing whereon to lean remains,

When strongholds crumble to dust;

When nothing is sure but that God still reigns

That is just the time to trust.

Tis better to walk by faith than sight

In this path of yours and mine;

And the pitch-black night, when there's no other light,

Is the time for our faith to shine."

God did not slay Job but brought him out of his sufferings with great benefits and blessings. After his ordeal he knew the God he loved in a far deeper way than he did before. In his own words he said,

> *"I have heard of thee by the hearing of the ear: but now mine eye seeth thee. Wherefore I abhor myself and repent in dust and ashes."* (Job 42:5)

He forgives his friends for their harsh treatment, prays for them and God restores his life; that is, his relationships, health and prosperity.

> *"And the LORD turned the captivity of Job, when he prayed for his friends: also the LORD gave Job twice as much as he had before. So Job died being old and full of days."* (Job 42:10, 17)

If a man of Job's wisdom and knowledge could put his faith and trust in the living God, surely we of the twenty-first century would be wise to do the same. The profound scientific truths revealed from the mouth of this godly man are only one aspect of his life. More important was his faith and personal relationship with God. If you know that you are not saved our doubt your salvation, will you follow Job's example and trust the Lord Jesus Christ as your Savior today? **Appendix 2** is a simple explanation of the gospel of Jesus Christ that will show you how to be saved.

# APPENDIX 2

## THE CHRISTIAN GOSPEL MESSAGE:

## INTRODUCING JOB'S SAVIOR

### How to Become a Christian

You can become a Christian by accepting Jesus Christ as your personal Lord and Savior. This is the most important decision you will ever make in your life. God sent His Son into this world 2000 years ago to receive the Kingdom, but man rejected Him and nailed Him to a cross. The crucifixion of Jesus Christ was not a defeat for God but a victory for mankind. Through His death, burial and resurrection the Son of God destroyed the power of Satan, the Devil. By dying on the cross and shedding His divine, sinless blood, Jesus Christ paid in full your debt of sin and through His resurrection, He guarantees you will be justified (declared not guilty before God) from sin's penalty if you repent of your sin and believe the gospel. He is the Redeemer that Job spoke of in his trial of suffering and in whom he had placed his faith. Job did not just hope in his Redeemer, but he <u>knew</u> his Redeemer. That's real salvation.

> *"For <u>I know</u> that my redeemer liveth, and that he shall stand at the latter day upon the earth: And though after my skin worms destroy this body, yet in my flesh shall I see God."* (Job 19:25-26)
>
> *Death, the grave and Hell held no power over Job because he would rise to stand before his Redeemer at the latter day. Neither do they hold any control over the sinner who puts his or her faith and trust in the Lord Jesus Christ. Jesus will raise His own again at the last day* (John 6:44)
>
> *"Jesus saith unto her, I am the resurrection, and the life: he that believeth in me, though he were dead, yet shall he live: And whosoever liveth and believeth in me shall never die. Believest thou this? She (Martha) saith unto him, Yea, Lord: I believe that thou art the Christ, the Son of God, which should come into the world."* (John 11:25-27)

Martha's Savior was the same as Job's. The Lord Jesus Christ invites you also to come and receive salvation today and take advantage of God's abundant mercy. The Bible not only reveals scientific truth; more importantly it shows clearly how to become a Christian. Rocks and mountains will pass away but your soul is eternal and more important than any thing in the world. The following verses explain how to be saved and know it.

1. *Understand that <u>you have sinned</u> and come short of God's perfect standard. He is Holy and you are a sinner. This is a fact as certain as any scientific law.*

> *"For all have sinned and come short of the glory of God."* (Romans 3:23)

2. *Recognize that God requires a penalty for sin. God must punish all people, whose sins have not been forgiven, including you. Your soul is under present condemnation.*

   *"For the wages of sin is death;"* (Romans 6:23a)

3. *The penalty for your sin is death and the fire of hell forever. You are lost in your present condition.*

Job and his generation believed in a fiery interior of the earth; a real hell, and a place of eternal suffering for sin for the never-dying souls of lost sinners. They identified it as down inside the earth where today's scientists recognize a partially-melted asthenosphere and plastic burning mantle, as well as a liquid outer core – all at extremely hot temperatures! They also believed in a redeemer who would save sinners from going there. The New Testament is full of warnings on hell, most given personally by Jesus Christ and also by His apostles. Jesus preached three times more about hell than about heaven. He should know because He created Hell for the devil and his angels, but not for man. It is that terrible! For example:

> *"It is high as heaven; what canst thou do? deeper than hell; what canst thou know?"* (Job 11:8)
>
> *"Hell is naked before him, and destruction hath no covering."* (Job 26:6)
>
> *"As for the earth, out of it cometh bread: and under it is turned up as it were fire."* (Job 28:5)

**Figure 2**

The Biblical teaching on Hell

*"And in hell he lifted up his eyes, being in torments, And he cried and said, send Lazarus, that he may dip the tip of his finger in water, and cool my tongue; for I am tormented in this flame."* (Luke 16:23a, 24d-g)

*"And death and hell were cast into the lake of fire. This is the second death. And whosoever was not found written in the book of life was cast into the lake of fire."* (Revelation 20:14-15)

4. *Realize that God loves you and wants to save you. He has provided a Sacrifice for your sin so that you can be forgiven and escape the penalty for your sin – hell and the lake of fire.*

The Father sent His sinless Son to earth to die on your behalf (as your Substitute). Jesus Christ bore your sins in His Body on the cross and paid their price in full with His Blood. Therefore, He is the Redeemer. He rose from the dead because the Father accepted His sacrifice for you. This is the substance of the gospel message that can save your soul. It is not complicated but you must understand clearly and respond through faith in order to be saved.

> *"For I delivered unto you first of all that which I also received, how that Christ died for our sins according to the Scriptures; And that he was buried, and that he rose again the third day according to the Scriptures:"* (I Corinthians 15:3-4)

5. *To be saved you must repent of your sin and personally receive Jesus Christ into your heart. Repentance is an 180$^0$ change of mind and direction in life, from sin and self to faith in the Lord Jesus Christ. From walking away from God you turn around and come directly to Him for salvation, and follow Him thereafter. It comes from the mind AND heart, and is an act of the will.*

> ***"I tell you Nay: but except ye repent ye shall all likewise perish."*** (Luke 13:3 & 5)

> *"Testifying both to the Jews, and also to the Greeks, repentance toward God, and faith toward our Lord Jesus Christ."* (Acts 20:21)

6. *Receive Jesus Christ now by calling upon Him to save you.*

> *"That if thou shalt confess with thy mouth the Lord Jesus, and shalt believe in thine heart that God hath raised Him from the dead, thou shalt be saved. For with the heart man believeth unto righteousness and with the mouth confession is made unto salvation."* (Romans 10:9-10)

Confess to God that you have sinned. Acknowledge that Jesus Christ is the Son of God and that He died and shed His Blood to pay for your sins, and resurrected for your justification. You will be personally justified (pardoned) when, by faith, you ask God to forgive your sin and invite Jesus Christ to come into your heart to be your Lord and Savior. God never turns anyone away. He came to save sinners.

> *"For whosoever shall call upon the name of the Lord shall be saved."* (Romans 10:17)

God promises definitely to save you because He states **you shall be saved** if you call on the Lord Jesus Christ. Salvation is not hoping but knowing that you are saved. Take this step of faith now and prove God's faithfulness. He will save you at once!

Then you will no longer fear death, the grave or Hell. You will have a home in Heaven and live forever with the Lord Himself and the saved who have passed on before you, and those who will follow in the future. Jesus invited people to accept salvation many times in the four gospels.

> *"Verily, verily I say unto you, He that believeth on me hath everlasting life."* (John 6:47)

7. *Becoming a Christian means possessing eternal life, and this life is a gift which cannot be lost. Once you are saved God keeps you as His child forever. Salvation is based on Christ's work, not yours.*

> *"And I give unto them eternal life; and they shall never perish, neither shall any man pluck them out of my hand."* (John 10:28)
>
> *"For by grace are ye saved through faith; and that not of yourselves: it is the gift of God: Not of works, lest any man should boast."* (Ephesians 2:8-9)

8. *Salvation is summed up in a few beautiful verses that many have believed to the saving of their souls. They are the sum and substance of Job's confession of faith in his redeemer.*

> *"For God so loved the world, that he gave his only begotten Son, that whosoever believeth in him should not perish, but have everlasting life."* (John 3:16)
>
> *"He that believeth on him is not condemned: but he that believeth not is condemned already, because he hath not believed in the name of the only begotten Son of God."* (John 3:18)
>
> *"Very, verily, I say unto you, He that heareth my word, and believeth on him that sent, hath everlasting life, and shall not come into condemnation; but is passed from death unto life."* (John 5:24)

Put your name in place of "the world," and in place of "whosoever," and you will recognize what Job's Redeemer has done for you. All you need do is accept what He has accomplished on the cross for you personally and you will be saved. Do it now because you have no guarantee of tomorrow.

> *"For what shall it profit a man, if he shall gain the whole world, and lose his own soul? Or what shall a man give in exchange for his soul?"* (Mark 8:36-37)

## After Becoming a Christian

1. *A newborn Christian needs to grow spiritually through the Word of God. You cannot grow without reading and obeying it. The Bible's Words are "spirit and*

*they are life."* (John 6:63) *Use the King James Bible. It is the pure and powerful Word of the Living God! That is WHY you can trust it when it speaks of science. How much more when it speaks of your spiritual needs!*

> *"As newborn babes, desire the sincere milk of the word, that ye may grow thereby:"* (I Peter 2:2)

2. *After being saved you need to be Biblically-baptized by immersion as a public testimony of your salvation, and then join a Bible-believing local church. The church is like a Christian family to the believer. It is the bride of Christ according to the Scriptures.*

> *"Then they that gladly received his word were baptized: and the same day there were added unto them (the Jerusalem Church) about three thousand souls."* (Acts 2:41)

3. *Christians grow in faith by obedience to the Lord's commands given in His Word. Serve the Lord by prayer (talking to God), witnessing for Christ (talking to others) and serving in your local church.*

> *"And they continued steadfastly in the apostles' doctrine and fellowship, and in breaking of bread (The Lord's Supper), and in prayers."* (Acts 2:42)

The Christian life is a wonderful relationship between you and your Savior. A Christian has a personal relationship with the living God. We know we are saved and that we belong to Him. We can appreciate His wonderful creation and marvel at His amazing works! Most importantly, we know beyond the shadow of a doubt that our sins are forgiven and we are going to Heaven when we die. What could be better than that? Come to Christ too!

# INDEX OF WORDS AND PHRASES

www.ingramcontent.com/pod-product-compliance
Lightning Source LLC
LaVergne TN
LVHW061247100826
845148LV00008B/1046

* 9 7 8 1 7 3 7 1 0 0 5 2 2 *